Subroto Bagchi was born in Patnagarh, Orissa, in 1957. He is co-founder and chief operating officer of MindTree Consulting, one of India's most admired companies. He was ranked among India's fifteen most influential business persons by *Business Today* magazine in 2006. He has been well known for his columns, 'Arbor Mentis', for *Businessworld*, and 'Times of Mind' for the *Times of India*. *The High-Performance Entrepreneur* is his first book. His other writing can be accessed at www.mindtree.com/subrotobagchi

Subroto Bagchi is married to Susmita, a writer, and they have two daughters, Neha and Niti.

PRAISE FOR THE BOOK

A must-read for anyone aspiring to start a new venture. You will find yourself referring often to this book as you chart your course forward on the exciting adventure of entrepreneurship.

—**Vijay Govindarajan**
Earl C. Daum Professor of International Business,
Tuck School of Business at Dartmouth College

Subroto Bagchi has converted his experience in building MindTree into a treasure trove of perspective and advice to the budding entrepreneur. Written in an easy conversational style, with examples, it provides a peek into the personal and team characteristics—persistence, integrity, passion and sacrifice—that result in high-performance entrepreneurship. A must-read for all who dream of building a great institution from scratch.

—**C.K. Prahalad**
Paul and Ruth McCracken Distinguished
University Professor,
The Ross School of Business,
The University of Michigan

THE HIGH-PERFORMANCE ENTREPRENEUR

Golden Rules for Success in Today's World

SUBROTO BAGCHI

PENGUIN
PORTFOLIO

PORTFOLIO

Published by the Penguin Group

Penguin Books India Pvt. Ltd, 11 Community Centre, Panchsheel Park, New Delhi 110 017, India

Penguin Group (USA) Inc., 375 Hudson Street, New York, New York 10014, USA

Penguin Group (Canada), 90 Eglinton Avenue East, Suite 700, Toronto M4P 2Y3

Penguin Books Ltd, 80 Strand, London WC2R 0RL, England

Penguin Ireland, 25 St Stephen's Green, Dublin 2, Ireland (a division of Penguin Books Ltd)

Penguin Group (Australia), 250 Camberwell Road, Camberwell, Victoria 3124, Australia (a division of Pearson Australia Group Pty Ltd)

Penguin Group (NZ), 67 Apollo Drive, Rosedale, North Shore 0632, New Zealand (a division of Pearson New Zealand Ltd)

Penguin Group (South Africa) (Pty) Ltd, 24 Sturdee Avenue, Rosebank, Johannesburg 2196, South Africa

Penguin Books Ltd, Registered Offices: 80 Strand, London WC2R 0RL, England

First published in Portfolio by Penguin Books India 2006
This paperback edition published 2008

Copyright © Subroto Bagchi 2006

All rights reserved

10 9 8 7 6 5 4 3 2

ISBN 9780143064268

Typeset in Minion Regular by SÜRYA, New Delhi
Printed at Deunique Printers, New Delhi

To the first five hundred MindTree Minds and in particular,
Ashok Soota
N. Krishna Kumar
S. Janakiraman
Scott Staples
Anjan Lahiri
Kamran Ozair
N. Parthasarathy
Kalyan Banerjee
and the baby of the team, Rostow Ravanan

Men who were ready to start.

Contents

Preface

I like to see myself as a journal-keeper of sorts. When MindTree Consulting was started with nine other co-founders in 1999, I felt that I had two duties. One, helping with the task of building the organization. Two, watching the process unfold, so that it could be narrated to people who could benefit from our experience and in turn launch their own endeavours.

It is in that context that my meeting with Sudeshna Shome Ghosh of Penguin proved to be a turning point. She wanted me to write a book based on the experience of setting up MindTree.

My first reaction was to look around to see what was already available. I was quite surprised to see that not much experiential and real-time material is on the bookshelves on a topic like this. You have the assorted management textbooks on entrepreneurship and a whole bunch of self-help books on various aspects of management. Then there is the enormous body of literature by people who have written success stories long after the success was born. Very little of it narrated in the first person by the people who actually did it. That told me, this book is needed.

It took me a year to write *The High-Performance Entrepreneur*. I do not claim to have provided profound knowledge. I have written it from my limited, and often unsophisticated, perspective.

I have a dream, though. Ten years from now, somewhere a person will say, his or her entrepreneurial voyage was helped in some small way by reading this book.

A book's strength lies not just in what is written in it. It is about what you could potentially take away from it. For I believe, the world goes round not on the strength of giving, but the ability to receive. I trust this ability in my readers will make up for the incompleteness of the book. It is such a vast subject, it is bound to be incomplete.

I am grateful to my colleagues at MindTree, particularly co-founder and Chairman Ashok Soota, who gave me the space to write this book.

Krishan Chopra, Executive Editor at Penguin, made valuable suggestions for changes. Shanti Uday, my Administrator at MindTree, joyfully helped out with the changes. To both, I am profoundly grateful.

The proceeds from this book will go to MindTree Foundation that works in the area of children's education with particular emphasis on the needs of children with disabilities.

Bangalore   *Subroto Bagchi*
1 September 2006

Introduction

There are an estimated 6.5 billion people on earth. Of these, a third live in India and China. In the Indian subcontinent alone, there are 450 million children below the age of 15 who will join the workforce soon. Neither the government nor large businesses can by themselves create avenues for employment and growth for these people. It can only be done by new entrepreneurs.

Entrepreneurs create jobs. Jobs provide people with livelihoods. Without a livelihood, every one of us is lost on this planet. Given a good source of livelihood, we feel secure enough to raise families and are able to provide emotional security to the people who depend on us, besides exploring our own potential. Thus developing entrepreneurship should be a matter of global priority.

Yet, until recently, the subject of entrepreneurship was never studied with any seriousness. That is changing. The Kaufmann Center for Entrepreneurial Leadership estimated in a winter 2001 report that the world over, more than 1400 colleges and universities offer some form of entrepreneurial education. More than $500 million is invested in endowed professorships and chairs on the subject. Entrepreneurship has arrived as a subject of study. Yet, no one learns its nuances by only going to a college any more than you can learn skydiving by watching a National Geographic film. The kid who has ever sold lemonade with mom's inventory knows more about customer interaction than a rookie MBA does.

Entrepreneurs are very focused and busy people. You will seldom find them writing a book on how to start a company. I felt obligated to do it so that it augments the emerging body of academic knowledge, with down-to-earth what worked for me and what did not kind of stuff.

This book is not about how to start a company. It is about creating high-performance entrepreneurs. High-performance entrepreneurship differs from the act of just starting something on your own and being self-employed. It differs in the level of its aspiration. Therefore, as the title suggests, this book is about how to start a company that has the potential to become a high-performance organization. A study of entrepreneurship presented at the First Annual Global Entrepreneurship Symposium by Dr Erko Autio showed that less than 5 per cent entrepreneurial ventures are likely to be called 'high potential'. According to the economist David Birch, 'high potential' companies, or 'gazelles', accounted for 70 per cent of job growth in the US between 1992 and 1996. In Sweden, seven out of ten new jobs are created by small, high-potential firms.

Having watched MindTree grow to 3500 people and cross $102 million in revenues, making it the first IT services company in India that made it in all of six years, I wanted to pass on to would-be entrepreneurs some of the skills needed to make a high-potential company a high-performance one. High-performance entrepreneurship is not an accident—it has to be planned that way.

In my life, I have been an entrepreneur thrice. Once, as a small kid, I sold balloons. As a grown-up, at the age of 28, I had my first taste of serious entrepreneurship. It lasted all of three years. At the age of 42, MindTree happened and it continues to happen. In-between, I worked for other people and helped build some really large and successful organizations. Even as a salaried employee in these organizations, my style of functioning was entrepreneurial. In that sense, even though MindTree is the largest single platform of my life's experience in entrepreneurship, I have nurtured many of the lessons right through. In this book, I frequently go back to tell you about what happened at MindTree. That name is to be seen as emblematic of the start-up experience. Only then can the valuable lessons be picked up with which even greater ships can set sail.

The most exciting thing about entrepreneurship is its capability to create jobs. Creating large-scale job opportunities through high-performance entrepreneurship is fine, but we all know that the exercise is fraught with great risk of failure. So, why do it? There are many good reasons.

High-performance entrepreneurs create great wealth. Not just for themselves but for others. Often they use the power of wealth to build a legacy for society at large. Behind the great educational system of the US, for instance, is a huge amount of personal wealth donated by entrepreneurs. Without their support some of the greatest initiatives to protect the world's heritage, our arts and literature and the environment would be difficult.

Entrepreneurs drive innovation. Innovation seldom comes from very large and established players. The reason is simple. Innovation disrupts the established way of things. Large, profitable organizations frown at disruptions. For innovative people, it is sometimes easier to start something ground-up.

Entrepreneurship can be deeply rewarding simply as a journey itself. The richness of experience and sheer self-confidence you get from starting a small shop is sometimes greater than running a huge department for an established entity. Nothing about entrepreneurship is spectator sport, many things in a paid job at a large corporation can be.

Entrepreneurship is a creative process and when done successfully, it can give you the highest sense of accomplishment possible. That sense of accomplishment is next only to having and raising your baby.

Last but not the least, the world has become an entrepreneur-friendly place like never before. There is no government in the world today that says we do not want peace and we do not want entrepreneurs. Funding is becoming global and, more importantly, resources are following ideas. There is a surfeit of angel funding, private equity and institutional venture capital funds today that are willing to provide risk capital to people with vision, ideas and commitment to build something new through sheer hard work.

Given all that, more people must start to think not just of starting their own enterprise, but starting it right, so that they can become high-performance entrepreneurs.

But, be informed—it is not for everyone. For hundreds

of enterprises that start, a handful make it to the finishing line—if there is a finishing line, that is! Of these, only a very small number would indeed qualify to become high performance by converting a start-up into a sustainable engine of growth through job and wealth creation. Yet, a closer look at an Apple, Intel or Infosys will tell you, none of these just happened. Their movement from being another start-up to becoming a high-performance entrepreneurship was most certainly planned with meticulous detail. They were engineered to be high performance.

Yet, it all begins at that special moment when someone gets an inner call that says, 'You are designed to create something new.'

Most aspiring entrepreneurs struggle internally to decipher if their special moment has arrived. So, let us discuss about the magic of that moment when you indeed realize that you are ready. At each stage, reflect and draw your own conclusions. Look around and read the signs. Who knows, you may be the next big success!

ONE

When Do I Know If I Am Ready?

Neil called me up one afternoon to seek time for a 'crucial discussion'. To me, it was a predictable conversation. Neil was in his late thirties, had worked his way up his company to become a program manager. His company is a world leader in semiconductor technology. Neil had joined as an R&D engineer and done very well in the first five years of his career. He was known to be one of the brightest engineers in the organization. In the next ten years, he diversified his portfolio and started taking up assignments that moved him from being an individual professional contributor to a group technical lead. Later, he handled the transition of the company, which was a technology bull-pen, to an orchestrated, process-compliant organization. This involved both discovery and frustration for him. He started to understand, and seek solutions to, many confounding aspects of R&D management. Now, clearly at the crossroads, he was thinking, what next? Hence the call.

I met Neil the following Saturday afternoon. The

discussion veered to his career options. He was clearly frustrated and wanted to do something on his own. As we chatted into the evening, I asked him what his personal goals were. Neil was, for most of his life, in the top percentile in compensation and benefits. His work had stagnated for the better part of the last five years but he had uncomplainingly pocketed the salary increases and perks that came with the job. His lifestyle included membership of some of the best clubs, playing tennis and golf over the weekends and the satisfaction of putting his two children through the best private school in town. He had overstretched himself in terms of home loan repayments, and thanks to his borrowing capacity, had purchased a second fancy apartment and a rather expensive car. Now he was contemplating starting a company on his own.

Neil understood the risks of doing something like that. He also knew that starting his own company could mean great upsides. But the critical first step needed to be an entrepreneur is the ability to make personal needs and comforts subservient to the larger organizational goals. No start-up could afford the kind of compensation that Neil enjoyed—he was overpaid for what he was doing, but that was another story! Despite the fact that he was at a career crossroad and was keen to give in to the entrepreneurial dream, he could not imagine cutting his own pay package to set up a company. Call it a deadly embrace, the inevitable comfort trap or whatever else you want to. Much as Neil was fantasizing about starting a company, the prospect of a lifestyle drop unnerved him. He pushed the idea out into the future.

I was clear in my head, Neil was not ready today—he would probably never be.

When we started MindTree, I was working with Lucent Technologies. The year was 1997, when the telecom world was moving like there was going to be no tomorrow. Lucent, spun off from AT&T, was a telecommunications giant and owned Bell Labs. Its share price had crossed $100 in the unprecedented boom of the 1990s. When Lucent wanted to set up an Indian operation, I moved over after spending ten years at Wipro. At Lucent, I was in a compensation trap very similar to Neil's. However, I never got caught in the clubbing and social climbing that went with such jobs. When we got to start MindTree, with me were people like Ashok Soota who was at the helm of Wipro's Information Technology business—as were co-founders Krishna Kumar and Janakiraman. The latter duo were chief executives of their respective divisions at Wipro. Each one of us, with the exception of Ashok, took a salary reduction of 40 per cent at the start of the company. Ashok took a salary reduction of 60 per cent. That was in 1999. In 2001, when the economy tanked, Ashok, Krishna Kumar and Janakiraman took an additional 25 per cent reduction and I took another 10 per cent. That was not reinstated well until the end of 2004. The market compensation of each individual, by that time, had become three to four times as much as what we earned at MindTree. However, our thinking was clear. If the leaders do not demonstrate frugality, it is very difficult to build the requisite culture in an upcoming organization. That must be borne out by demonstrated behaviour right at the top. Yes, this could mean giving up on the fancy car, a drastic reduction in spend money or personal time. But that is the way you build wealth. Comfort with postponed gratification is a critical requirement of entrepreneurship.

Besides Neil's, I am reminded of two other examples. One is that of Vincent and the other Ismail's. Vincent, like Neil, met me once to discuss a hot new product idea that he felt very passionate about. We discussed at length why I did not think the product idea was sustainable. Unlike Neil, Vincent had pretty much decided to leave his company and had even gone ahead and told his boss. Having told him that I did not think much of the software framework that he wanted to make a product out of, I also told him that I was not an authority on the subject and that he should talk to more informed people. He was accompanied by two of his colleagues who shared his burning desire to start a company. He was not disheartened by the conversation with me, but he did dishearten me with what he had to say at the end of the conversation. As the trio was leaving, Vincent stopped near the door, excused himself from his two colleagues and asked to see me alone for a moment. 'Assuming that I gave the idea a try and failed, do you think you could hire me at MindTree?' he asked.

I was shocked at his poor resilience and even more so at the lack of integrity he displayed. On the one hand, he thought he had a path-breaking idea based on which he would change the world. On the other hand, faced with the smallest obstacle, he was ready to give up, reserving his place in the queue for the parachute! Worse, he did not feel awkward keeping his collaborators at the door to strike a private deal for a safety net with me. Clearly, Vincent was not ready—nor would he ever be.

Ismail, unlike Neil and Vincent, actually started his own company at the height of the dotcom boom. Though he was a talented and capable professional who was doing well for himself in the corporate world, his biggest problem was his inability to balance his professional priorities with his personal ones. He was married to an extremely attractive woman who was given to the creature comforts of life and a large part of Ismail's efforts were directed towards keeping her happy. So, what did Ismail do to buy her support for his new phase in life? With the avowed purpose of housing engineers who must work late to write code, Ismail first rented a guest house and then appointed a company cook, who for all practical purposes was to cook for his wife! With that, Ismail subordinated organizational goals to domestic peace. A few years after, the company drove itself into the ground.

The characters in each of the three narratives are fictional, their stories are not. Each of the examples indicates how little prepared the individuals were to build an organization. If even remotely, the thought of a safety net haunts you and you cannot talk yourself out of it, you are not yet ready to set sail. When you build an organization, your own comforts must be subordinate to all other interests. Finally, there cannot be thoughts of exit options in the event of a failure.

One must remember that failure cannot be an option when you raise money from others or take on employees who work to make the shared vision a reality. This is not to say that you and you alone are responsible for all the success and unless you are very sure of success, do not start a company. Sometimes failure is forced upon the entrepreneur by external factors. For every organization that succeeds, countless others have to fail. That is the rule of the game. Yet, failure cannot weigh on your mind so much that you become tentative in your search for success. While we are on that topic, it is worthwhile to draw a checklist for preparedness. Here is a set of questions, whose answers will help you to decide if unlike the characters from my past, you are ready to start.

Would I feel lost if my boss found out my desire to venture out and gave me the pink slip?

Have I discussed the venture and the possible outcomes with my dependants?

Am I ready to give up my house, car, club membership and official position?

Would I be willing to take a serious salary cut to make sure the company is not saddled with a fat compensation structure—and thereby can break even sooner?

Would I be happy travelling economy class as against the business class travel I am so accustomed to as a vice president in a multinational corporation?

Will it be fine with me to stay in a modest hotel and travel by train and not taxi?

Is it all right for others in the company to earn more than me?

Am I willing to work 70 hours a week for the next few years to make sure the company stands on its own?

Will I be comfortable in working out of a cheap business

centre or from a downmarket address, with bad air-conditioning, hired furniture, poor lighting and no secretaries?

Will I be comfortable making my own phone calls, writing my own memos and creating my own set of slides?

Will I be able to set my own goals and work unsupervised?

Will I feel awkward going back to people who reported to me a long time ago to solicit business?

When we started MindTree, I was once asked by a roomful of analysts why I co-founded MindTree. I was taken aback by the obvious nature of the question as much as by my lack of preparedness to answer. I could have given them a clichéd reply that years of management training equips you with and I am sure at least some of the reasons would have worked. Instead, I heard myself tell them something from my gut. I told them that starting a company is like deciding to have a baby. Ask most women and they will tell you that there can never be a rational enough reason to get into the problems of bearing a baby. It is a very difficult task, full of discomforts and sacrifices. Yet, when the time comes, a woman would give up everything in the world to be able to bear her child. No pain, no discomfort, no change in lifestyle daunts her from becoming a mother.

Starting your own enterprise is a little like motherhood. You know it when the time has come and you waive all caution and comfort to embrace the little sign of life deep inside you and you would do everything—*everything*—to bring it into the world.

Having said that, sometimes people think of starting their own enterprise for the wrong reasons.

All the wrong reasons

This one will sound familiar to most readers. 'We are three good friends and we have this fantastic idea. We want to start a company. Tell us how.'

Being great friends and having a fantastic idea indeed constitute some of the necessary conditions for starting a company, but in themselves, they are not sufficient.

Many great companies have been built by friends. Having said that, personal friendship can also come in the way of creating great organizations. Apple, Intel and Infosys are great examples of how professional friendship provided the nurturing ground on which memorable companies were built.

At the same time, we know myriad examples where familiarity bred contempt and not only did the companies go haywire, so did the relationships. When friends come together, they need to put the commitment to build an organization ahead of the joy of togetherness. They need to ask each other many difficult questions before they embark on the journey. Later in the chapter, we will look at some of these questions that friends would do well to ask themselves before signing up.

*

The second most common folly is in thinking that a great idea for a new gizmo is all that it takes to build a high-performance organization.

It is true that the formidable GE (2005 revenue: US $150 billion) was built after Thomas Edison invented the light bulb. It is also true that Microsoft started with a bought-out operating system called DOS and then augmented it to supply PCDOS to IBM for the personal computer that the company launched in 1981. Apple started with a small computer when Steve Wozniak and Steve Jobs put together a few printed circuit boards and created the first Apple. Intel was started by Gordon Moore and Andy Grove with the world's first four-bit microprocessor chip called the PPS4. Yet, a close examination of these companies will tell you that no enterprise gets built on the strength of a single great product idea.

The idea behind a new way of creating sliced bread, a faster-acting mousetrap or a so-called 'killer-app' may look earth-shaking in its potential. Yet, time consumes all. From the Model 'T' Ford to PPS4. So, while having a fantastic idea is a great starting point, unless there is a reasonable view of what larger business the company can be in, the life of an enterprise can be very short-lived.

Visualizing a vision of that potential is what high-performance entrepreneurship is all about, even as it is difficult to have a truly long-term view of what products or services your company could get into five years from now.

In 1996, I was visiting Sony's corporate office in Tokyo. On the ground floor, all the products that Sony has ever created are showcased in the order of their birth. At the very end of the display chain at the time that I was visiting was the high-definition television. This, in 1996, was frontier technology. At the beginning of the display line was Sony's first, albeit failed, product. Can you imagine what it was? It was a wooden rice-cooker. When Sony launched it, there were no takers.

Companies, like ideas, have a life of their own. A founder who thinks that one potentially great invention is a good reason to start a company needs to introspect. Is it a great idea in itself or is it the vision of a family of ideas? The recipes for the two, the talent required to make them work and the investments needed are very different. If you have invented a great product, you could just sell it or settle for an internal honour by filing a patent for the organization you work for. Building an organization that will spawn one great idea after another is a very different proposition from inventing one great product.

No, I am not discouraging someone who has a great idea and wants to start something on his own. But you should know that if you do not have a greater vision and accompanying commitment, you may run out of steam very soon.

Building a company is not like planting one giant tree. It is about creating an entire forest some day. You may not know exactly how. You may not have the remotest idea of where the know-how and the resources will come from. Yet, you must live that thought, you must be exhilarated by the prospect of doing it. Only then will you be willing to pay the price, brace the ups and downs and draw strength from the size of the dream when everything around you threatens to crumble.

*

This one is the popular mid-life peeve: My career is not getting anywhere. I hate this company and I do not like the boss. I want to start a company.

Take a deep breath. Think. Talk to your spouse. Talk to a friend you have not met in a long time. Ask these people if they think you are ready to start a company. You may have a change of heart after the conversation. Chances are that you are ready to change jobs within the same company. You may even be ready to change companies.

There could even be a great reason to change the *you* in yourself first. For many people nudging their forties and knocking at their proverbial mid-life, overhauling the engine may be the greater need of the day.

People often start a great journey from a negative experience. Consider Mahatma Gandhi. He was travelling by first class in a train in South Africa when a white conductor challenged him because only whites were supposed to travel by first class. Gandhi argued in vain that he had a first-class ticket. The angry conductor threw him and his luggage on a dark platform at the next station and the train left without him. That was Gandhi's first taste of apartheid. Many historians will tell us, in that moment, freedom was conceived. I believe that Gandhi's great achievement was not propelled by his dislike of the white man who threw him out. There was a higher call and a more abundant justification for liberating India with the power of non-violence.

Do you see the South African train conductor in your boss every time you meet him? Has the system thrown you on the platform yet? When we give birth to a great idea that gets converted into an institution, there has to be a greater reason than just the stress of our circumstances.

I always like to think of Mother Teresa as one of the

greatest entrepreneurs of our time. She started with an angel investment of five rupees in 1948 from the Archbishop of Calcutta. By the turn of the century, her Missionaries of Charity had 602 homes in 125 countries and her band of 4000 sisters from as many as forty different national origins marched to the same mission, vision and core values. How did she build that institution? What was the impetus? Disease and death that crawled in the gutters of Calcutta and nudged her saree each time she walked past? Was it the negative energy of her surroundings? Or was it the possibility of positive outcomes? Of spreading love, joy, seeing a dying destitute as an angel of peace?

It wasn't the former. She was to recall later that she had, in fact, 'received' her call. That was the starting point for Mother to move from Loreto Convent to the small rented house on Lower Circular Road in Calcutta where she and eight other sisters 'co-founded' the Missionaries of Charity.

Sometimes our push to move out of our current assignment, boss or company becomes too strong to ignore. Yet, in the absence of a higher call, the push factor is just like the experience Gandhi had on the night he was thrown out on the railway platform. It was a necessary but not sufficient condition to launch his movement.

*

I once met a 26-year-old engineer who wanted to get started without being clear about what he would do. What goods or services would he make? Who would he sell to? How would he ever make money and why would anybody be his customer? He had not thought any of these through. All he was telling me was: 'Oh, but if not now—when? My time is running out!'

With five years of work experience behind him, all he had done was write software code for which someone else had created the specifications. In a very serious vein, I told him to get a girlfriend, get married and raise a family, learn intensely for a few more years, rotate a few jobs, expose himself to sales, marketing and business finance and only then start his company. He was dejected for a moment. Then, to show me how strongly he was seized with the idea, he repeated, 'But time is running out.' Just because you feel the time is now or that time is running out is not reason enough to start a company.

In reality, *the time is now* only if you have the mission, vision and values worked out. The *time is now* if you have put together a team who share your personal values. The *time is now* if you are confident of your ability to envision a future and have the commitment to create a 'family' of products or services and not just a single invention. The *time is now* if you have the ability to raise an adequate amount of money. The *time is now* if at a personal level you think that you will be able to dedicate the time and energy needed. The *time is now* if your spouse and family approve of your decision to take the plunge and face uncertainty for the next ten years. That is often how long it takes to build a company right.

Sometimes, I come across altruistic people who tell me this strange line: 'I do not need the money, I want to do it for the country.'

If you do not need the money, do not start a company. It is that simple. There are many other ways to serve the country. You may not have a selfish view of what you would do if you made a lot of money. But you must be excited about the idea of making money. If you do not love money, it is unlikely that you will ever understand the nuances of generating wealth. It is unlikely that you will ever know the difference between a paying customer and an admirer of your work. You will not know the importance of cost management, of the obligation of an enterprise to generate tangible value for its stakeholders.

Profitability is a social obligation of enterprise. When companies fail on a large scale, economies and lives are destroyed. So, if you do not love money, stay right where you are and continue making the great contribution you are making right now.

I have no wish to overromanticize the concept of people starting their own companies. We need great entrepreneurs. But we also need equally great people, in much larger numbers, who will run the enterprises, take them beyond the wooden rice-cooker stage of Sony. While the focus of this book is to encourage people to start their own enterprise, one must also be aware that creating a company is not child's play.

When you build a company, you assume responsibility for your investors. You assume responsibility for the people who will buy your goods and services and use them. You assume responsibility towards all the good men and women who will work along with you to achieve your vision of growing a forest with the little sapling you hold in your hands today. You cannot put your personal, often transitional, desire to find alternative fulfilment ahead of the needs of all these people.

Having said all that and assuming that one has all the right reasons, the next question aspiring entrepreneurs ask is, 'Am I entrepreneur material?'

TWO

Profile of an Entrepreneur

It is interesting that before getting down to writing this book, the subject never occurred to me. Is there something like an entrepreneurial profile? I have not come across any significant body of work that concisely proposes the subject, nor have I seen a psychometric test that could tell us whether any of us is entrepreneur material or not. Is there something in common between GE's Thomas Alva Edison, Microsoft's Bill Gates, the Tata's Jamsetji Tata, Dell's Michael Dell, Wal-Mart's Sam Walton and Sony's Akio Morita? When we look at their lives closely, we do see some important traits. Anyone wanting to venture out should assess whether or not he has some of those traits. In this chapter, let me list a set of characteristics without which venturing out may not be advisable. Yet, I must caution, there are exceptions to every rule. But, exceptions they are.

Self-confidence: It is the # 1 attribute

The foremost attribute of people who become entrepreneurs is self-confidence. I would even argue that there are no exceptions to this rule. You cannot show me a person who does not believe in herself and yet is a successful entrepreneur. However small may be the size of the endeavour, self-confidence is the most critical ingredient of success. What is self-confidence? It is difficult to define it, but most people will be able to judge whether they have it by doing a little introspection.

It is something that either you have or do not, at a *given point in time*. The reason I am using the qualifier is that it is possible to build self-confidence and it is equally possible to lose it due to circumstances.

However, if at the time of starting out on your own you do not have a sustained phase of self-confidence, I would advise against venturing out. Wait for the right time.

Self-confidence can come from personal experience. As a little boy of six, I had gone to visit my maternal uncle. It was a time of great festivity in Berhampur, in West Bengal, where they lived. It was time for Durga Puja and in every locality, the idol of Durga was instated. We spent most of our time hanging around the community idol and there I found an older boy selling balloons. For some reason, he offered me apprenticeship. Without knowing what I was getting into, I accepted. To my delight, I found people quite willing to buy from me. It was quite easy and I made quite a bit of money. But when it was time to return home, I became worried. How would I explain the source of my income? What if my mother got angry with me for selling balloons? For a six-year-old who has done something without prior permission, this can be a huge issue. I had liked the whole experience of selling someone a balloon and having a repeat customer when a mother or a sister of a kid returned for more was exhilarating.

Selling balloons is a value-added activity. You buy the balloons, you breathe air into them, you carry them in a lot and you talk price with real customers. I do not quite remember how I handled the issue at home, but the next day, I was back in business.

From then on, when I look back at my life, I see a series of things that told me, I could *do it*. I would sign up for sports and debating and theatre and music and any other contest going on. It baffled me when I was thrown out of an audition for the school's annual day celebrations. I was so musically deaf that I did not know why they were rejecting me. So what? I had no shame in trying one more time in another school the next year.

By the time I was thirteen, my family had moved to another town. For some reason, I did not like the school there. I convinced everyone at home that I needed to go back to my old school. Leaving them behind, I headed back. My father, who had retired by then, finally agreed to come and stay with me till I completed the high school term. I was setting my directions—not someone else.

As a child, I was asthmatic, but I did not let that come in the way of physical activity. At eighteen, I got selected for parachute jumping as a cadet in the National Cadet Corps and trained with the Indian Army for two months. During the rigorous training, there were times I thought I would die. I never told anyone that I was asthmatic. They would not have selected me if I had. But the daily regimen of army exercise, their generous diet and the eventual five jumps cured my asthma.

When I came back, I felt I had become an adult and needed a sweetheart. So, at nineteen, I found her—all of sixteen years—got her to agree to be my beloved and promptly notified everyone at home. In India of 1975, you did such things at your own risk.

In 1976, I graduated from college and joined the local university for my Masters. Sixty days through the course, I decided that it was a waste of time. Moreover, I did not want to be a burden on my two brothers, who were supporting retired parents, another brother and me. So, I talked to my professor, left college and took up the job of a clerk in a government office. Only after getting my appointment letter did I notify my family that I had given up college.

A year after, I found my first real job, as a management trainee in DCM, at that time India's seventh largest business house. Once I got there, I worked my way up. During all this and at all of twenty-two, I figured out that I had to marry my sweetheart, and did so. In the process, I irked my in-laws and also jumped the queue of one immediate elder brother and a dozen older cousins. Not the practice in my generation. But who cared?

There is a reason why I am sharing these personal details with my readers. Looking back, these incidents at different points in time tell me the level of my own self-confidence.

If you looked back at your life, you would be able to see many small things, significant nonetheless, that hold the key. Strung together, they show your level of self-confidence.

To determine your entrepreneurial streak, ask yourself

if you tried out unusual things, and whether you enjoyed them.

Did you take the important decisions in your life or did someone else invariably take them for you?

Did you enjoy the process, irrespective of the outcome?

How well did you handle small adversities and who took decisions for you at that time?

Did you ever feel helpless?

Did you get out of the situation by taking your own decisions or did you allow the situation to determine the course?

Can you make friends with a stranger?

Do you know your physical and mental limitations? Do you think you can work to overcome them?

Do you feel comfortable in talking about yourself?

Do you feel comfortable asking others for help?

Does the act of buying and selling excite you?

Do you like meeting people?

Do you see things to completion?

Entrepreneurs value their sense of freedom, but they are also very disciplined

First of all, a clarification. Most successful career managers value their sense of freedom. In fact, organizations that recognize this and are willing to pay the price for it, breed a very special kind of manager, one who is like an entrepreneur in his area of operation.

All my life, both on the personal and the professional fronts, I have enjoyed being free to set my goals and create and work towards my own work plan and take my own decisions. I like taking instructions from more competent people and my customers. But I do not like someone telling me how to go about doing my work. I work best when I am given what is called a 'porous boundary'. When I look back at all the jobs that I did well, I see a common thread. Each one allowed me an enormous amount of freedom to do what I wanted to do.

This, however, comes with great responsibility. One is responsible for ensuring that one's stakeholders are delivered a beneficial outcome, if not always, at least most of the time. One is responsible, particularly, for customers and employees. Freedom is not lack of answerability. Many people mistake freedom with the absence of accountability. Freedom to me is the ability to explore and settle options the way I think is suitable and the ability to work within porous boundaries.

Sometimes people think that freedom for a business person is about deciding for yourself when to come and go, who to serve or not, how much to pay yourself, how much to be able to spend on entertainment, choosing the hotel you want to stay at or accounting for a personal trip as official.

None of these are about freedom. If you ask people who know, they will tell you that such attributes are severely looked down upon by successful entrepreneurs.

A good entrepreneur is a highly disciplined person.

Freedom to such an individual is an inner need for space in which the person can create greater value without interference. That process of creating greater value often involves risks, of trying creative ideas to stay ahead. He does not enjoy someone pulling him from behind or asking for a progress report by breathing down his neck every now and then.

This does not mean entrepreneurs are not accountable.

At MindTree, people routinely question us on policies, issues and directions. Every month, Ashok Soota, chairman of the company, sends out an electronic update called Snapshots. Every quarter, we meet all MindTree Minds for what is known as 'What's on your mind' and people put us on the mat. Every quarter, the board reviews and questions us—five of the nine members on the board are external directors who pore over an average 100 pages of reports and ask detailed and often uncomfortable questions on strategy and direction. In addition to all this, we are answerable to the government agencies and financial institutions of every country in which we operate. And, of course, we are answerable to the analysts who track us, press persons who seek our views and write about us, industry associations whose members we are. We are answerable for high-value purchases to even our suppliers and last but not the least, in a very real sense, we are answerable to our customers.

So, what is left? And what is this talk about freedom?

Freedom to an entrepreneur is the ability to choose a line of business and set goals consistent with stakeholder ambitions. Freedom is the ability to write and revise a business plan. Freedom is the ability to make a decision on a given product and service strategy. Freedom is about the ability to choose from whom you want to take money, on what terms. Freedom is the ability to decide whom you want to hire for what job. Freedom is the ability to settle policy that will govern the internal working of the organization. Freedom is the ability to say that the debate rests here and the decision begins.

Freedom is also about reaping the risks and the rewards that come from all this, but within the articulated guidelines of a business.

Entrepreneurs work hard and are extremely goal oriented

How do we quantify hard work? When I was working at Wipro, my last assignment was to work for chairman Azim Premji as corporate vice president, mission: quality. This was preceded by three other jobs in the organization. In the course of each, I had made a mark. I always used to think that I worked hard.

So, when I was being considered for the position, Premji asked me, how many hours a week do you put in? Not a superfluous question, this. The man measures and tracks the number of hours he works every week. He does not expect everyone in the organization to work as hard as himself. But he has figured out the minimum number of hours a person must be comfortable working in order to be part of his team. That number is a minimum of 60 hours a week, in reality closer to 70. Premji averages 80 hours a week. That is hard work. But just so we know, Premji never asks someone to change holiday plans, once these have been approved, never recalls someone on vacation.

Ashok Soota, chairman and managing director of MindTree, works as hard. He measures the number of days he is on travel every year. That number, when he was 62, was an average of 140 days a year. It does not mean that he is a workaholic with no life outside of work. He settles his vacation dates at the beginning of the year and these are non-negotiable. At least one vacation in the year involves a mountain trek or a snorkelling trip during which we do not contact him. Ashok's self-discipline and hard work rub off on every senior person in the organization. At the next level, a 70-hour workweek and an average 140 days of travel has been the way for all of us since MindTree was born.

Along with hard work, comes the ability to work unsupervised. It is a critical requirement of entrepreneurship. As a paid professional, often someone can blame the system for not providing either the direction or the resources. As an entrepreneur, you no longer have that latitude. You have to work hard, very hard.

That is why venture capitalists have coined the term 'sweat equity', the ownership that comes by the sweat of your brows.

Entrepreneurs are flexible, opportunistic and recognize the power of 'emergence'

I love this story about IBM and its founder Thomas Watson, Sr. that I heard Peter Drucker narrate. It was 1934 or '35. IBM had built the first accounting machines for banks but in the Depression years, no bank was buying anything. IBM was on the brink of bankruptcy. Watson's wife forced him to accompany her to a social event where he was seated next to a middle-aged lady.

While talking with her, Watson described to her the machine IBM had built. It turned out that the lady was in-charge of the library system in New York City. She told Watson that they were in complete disarray, unable to manage their books, and told him that she would need half a dozen of these! Next day, he sold her five of the machines.

Until that moment, Watson had never thought of his computing devices as machines for tracking books.

That one sale pulled IBM from the brink of bankruptcy.

Had it not been for Watson's capability to go with the emergent flow of events—moving from accounting machines to the recognition that he could make general purpose computers—IBM would not be what it is today. We all know that the essence of entrepreneurial ability is about building a future and living in it. Sometimes, it is about 'willing' a course for the enterprise. Yet, things do not always go the way you plan. Destiny tests you all the time, plays pranks and shows tiny openings in a moss-covered brick wall behind which often a whole new world awaits.

When we started MindTree and were a no-name entity in the US, a chance meeting took place with a man called Larry Kinder who had just moved in as CIO of Avis. We won an assignment to build consensus between two groups of Avis managers on the future of their on-line reservation system. A team from MindTree, led by Erik Mann, who is one of our best consultants, delivered well. Consequently, we moved on to win the technical design for re-architecting Avis.Com. Then we built the on-line reservation system. Today, the system handles $1 billion worth of transactions at Avis. In the course of following up on that small opening at Avis, we saw three CIOs come and go and then came a CEO who even wanted us out of the door. We survived all those changes and focused on building value, one day at a time.

Many analysts ask me how we won Avis. One morning,

Joe King—an early member of the MindTree team and currently a senior vice president of our US operations— called Larry Kinder's office at 7 in the morning. That is called the 'golden hour'. It is a direct marketer's dream time. The golden hour is when a senior executive has come in but his secretary has not—someone who is paid to block unwanted callers. Larry picked up the phone that day, listened to Joe's pitch and agreed to see us. I am sure he was used to a hundred such unsolicited calls—this was the heyday of the Internet boom. I often ask myself, what would have happened if Larry had not been in office that day? Why did he have to pay attention to Joe? What if he had dismissed that one call?

Providence is very powerful in our journeys and entrepreneurs must make room for her. It is not always what you bring to the table. Sometimes, it is an unexplainable turn of events that changes your course. From a small assignment for Larry in 1999, in 2006 MindTree did $15 million worth of business for the whole of the Cendant Group that owns Avis and learnt enough about the travel industry to start a vertical focused on it.

After Larry Kinder moved to a larger role at Cendant, due to turbulence in the organization, things became difficult for us. At the Avis end, a turnaround CIO named Raj Rawal took over. As it often happens in times of corporate transition, Raj had received mixed messages about our capability, role and contributions. My first meeting with him was not in happy circumstances. Yet, the moment I met Raj, something about him told me that I could bet everything for this man. We hit it off and under his leadership, the reorganization and our role in it got sorted out. Our relationship grew. In time, Raj moved on and eventually took over as CIO at Burger King. As he settled into his new job, the phone rang at my desk.

In 1999, we had started the company with the vision to be focused on two businesses: IT consulting and software services, and R&D services. The former was for building Internet-based applications and on the R&D side, we wanted to work on providing solutions in the telecom domain. In just about a year, there was a dotcom bust and the telecom domain just about vanished.

On the IT services side, we had to rapidly move into other areas like Supply Chain, Data-warehousing, Mainframe-based Application Management Services (AMS) and Enterprise Resource Planning (ERP). None of these words existed in the original business plan we had written. On the R&D side, we created new verticals like Semiconductors, Appliances, Industrial Automation and Avionics, Storage Technologies and Computing Platforms. Again, these were things we never thought we would dabble in. All that had to be done without losing the original positions of strength, all that had to be done in real time and by taking all our people along with us.

Nine out of ten companies born at the same time as us, anywhere in the world, do not exist today. Entrepreneurship requires the ability to read patterns on the wall, flexibility and an uncanny ability to seize the moment.

Entrepreneurship is about egolessness

Many people want to start companies in the prime of their careers, often after winning accolades as professional managers in large companies. That is great, but when you start your own company, you must know that you leave your past behind.

That is easier said than done.

A person's corporate success often comes from the power of the chair he sits on. He often underestimates how much he is an extension of that artefact. So, when that person steps out, the world repositions him without his knowing.

People have a hard time coping with the attendant loss of identity. The day you step out of the collared existence of a blue-chip company, you are a mongrel. The first thing you have to do is to forage and run and duck and breed and forage some more.

In all this foraging, you will come up against strangers. Some will love you for reasons you will never be able to fathom. Some will be brutal with you.

I remember fondly a meeting with an irate customer. He demanded that I see him immediately and I took a late-night flight from New York all the way to California and showed up at the appointed time. I stood outside his glass door while he remained busy on the phone for a full forty-five minutes—all the time knowing very well that I was standing there. When he finally showed me in, he did not apologize. The one-hour meeting was largely a one-sided rebuke. He did not offer me a glass of water or a coffee. After I came out, for a fleeting moment, I felt hurt. This man, in my past life would have had to take an appointment to see me—that is what my ego informed me. In the very next moment I realized that this was a set-up by destiny to prune me.

I am sure when a rose bush is pruned, it does not like the experience. But without the pruning, it will not give great blooms. In the early years of setting up shop, one has to budget for a lot of pruning.

Sales people learn this early in their careers. Sometimes with reason and sometimes quite mindlessly, people keep them waiting, shut the door on them, or are otherwise rude. As you grow up, you learn to deal with such responses, one way being not to take things personally. Even service engineers learn to deal with rejection. But most people who come from other areas of expertise, specially senior people, become quite shaken when they face such experiences. The worst thing that you could do is return the volley. Sometimes, life is just testing your ability to weather storms. Even if you are entrepreneur material, possessing patience, resilience, empathy and politeness in very difficult situations, the sense of rejection can lead to occasional self-pity. That is the last thing you need in such situations, to even think, 'when I was a senior executive at my last organization, this man would not dare deal with me like this'. The 'senior executive' and your 'last organization' are past and best treated as fiction. This man is the current reality and is best treated as someone who may be holding the key to your future.

One day, very early in our existence, I went to General Motors (GM) with Sandeep Sabharwal, at that time a sales director in the US, to make a sales presentation. The fact of the matter is that GM's IT outsourcing runs into billions of dollars and every large IT services company camps inside and outside GM's Detroit office. The giant EDS, a business and technology solutions company, was born out of GM.

And here was I, with less than 500 people and under $20 million in size, making a spirited pitch to explain why we were good enough for them. After a half-hour of involved presentation, I asked the gentleman from the purchase department what he thought of our proposal. He cleared his throat and said, 'You are so small that GM could chew you and spit you out before you knew it.' I laughed, but inside it hurt.

Sandeep and I stepped out, brought ourselves brownbag lunches and headed out to the next port of call. We were to meet someone at the Automobile Association of America (AAA). It took us some serious ego massages to be able to repeat the dog-and-pony show at the AAA, where too, in all probability, the prospect was ready to chew us up and throw us out. As we settled into the conference room with some effort to raise the spirit, I again started to explain who MindTree was and what it was about. To my surprise, the client just took over and told us that he knew about us and how high in his esteem we were as an organization. He had learnt all about us from his previous stint at Citibank, during which he had come to India as part of a delegation. He had met Ashok very briefly and was absolutely sold on MindTree. It was balm on a bruised ego after the rejection at GM. Sandeep and I told ourselves that our man at the AAA was the reality and the gentleman at GM was just another bad sales call.

Shortly after, I learnt that the gentleman at AAA had left his job. Another corporate reorganization! That apart, as of today, we are still to do business with AAA. The gentleman at GM is probably still there somewhere but through some other opening, we actually do business with one of the GM companies. So, acceptance and rejection are equally transitory, result in equally unpredictable outcomes and must be treated with equanimity, without involving your ego in the results.

Finally, another point about egolessness. Till yesterday, you flew business class, had a secretary make appointments for you and checked in at the choicest hotels. When you start out on your own, for a long time you will have to forget all that.

Investor money is meant to bring in customers, build and deliver products and services and generate cash before you start leading a life of such luxury. So, being economical with your expenses becomes critical to success. Six years into MindTree, none of us fly business class—with the exception of Ashok. All of us pick hotels at $50 or less on priceline.com whenever we travel overseas.

While we do all that, our colleagues whom we left behind in earlier organizations are entitled to great creature comforts. We know that postponed gratification is the essence of ownership. Hence, we do not compare ourselves with what we have left behind.

Entrepreneurs love money

If you do not love to make money, do not start a business. You will hear that many times over from me.

I meet a lot of people who love technology, so they want to start a company. I meet a lot of people who tell me that they have earned enough in their life and now want to set up a company to 'give something back'. None of these people will ever make great entrepreneurs. Sometimes, we think love for money is all about spending power. Some people have disdain for money because they associate money with being consumerist. In the hands of a creator of wealth, it is not always so. Some people use wealth to build more wealth. Some people like to make money so that they can change the state of things around them. Some enjoy the recognition and some just get a sense of high.

Some people have a deep need to build a legacy and see wealth as the way to do so. John D. Rockefeller's wealth created many legacies in many walks of life. The most memorable contribution made by him was the Rockefeller Foundation that started in 1913. In 2004, the foundation's assets stood at $2.4 billion, and in that year it disbursed grants, fellowships and programmatic funds worth $124 million. Jamsetji N. Tata, born in a family of clerics, seeded a business empire in 1859, just two years after India's first war of independence. In 2004 his Tata empire stood at $12.8 billion in size, and spanned 93 companies in seven businesses.

A lesser known fact is that 65.8 per cent of the empire is owned by charitable trusts. The Bill and Melinda Gates Foundation is arguably the world's second richest charitable organization with assets that stood at $26.9 billion in 2006. In each of these instances, the founders were guided by a sense of legacy. It became the deep driving desire behind growing their enterprise so as to make their names remembered by posterity. Without affection for wealth, men like Rockefeller, Gates and Tata could not have created their legacy.

In the Hindu pantheon, wealth is granted by a goddess

named Lakshmi. She is extremely jealous and possessive. She does not come to those who treat her as if she is incidental. Even if you manage to bring her in on some pretext, mythology has it that she flees at the smallest act of neglect. So, if someone says money is not my prime motivator, know that the goddess is listening.

THREE

Sensing the Right Opportunity

What business should you get into? I wish I knew how to tell you about this all-important subject. The truth is, I cannot, and I suspect that nobody can.

All I can tell you is that behind any high-performance entrepreneurship are invariably two things—a great idea that leads to a family of ideas, and solid implementation. As I told you in the beginning itself, just one great idea of a product or service, however path-breaking it may be, is unlikely to lead towards building an institution unless it evolves into a family of ideas.

Illustratively, the founders at Intel were deeply excited about the power of microprocessors and not just the PPS4 chip. So, a potential business model must go beyond an 'aha' idea. An 'aha' idea is about the power of invention, and by itself, may not be adequate to create an organization. A lot of inventive people are out there, and some of the things they bring to the world change the way we all work and live and play. Many new and established businesses benefit from such inventions. But to think that the inventor could equally succeed as an entrepreneur, and a high-performance one at that, is a long shot.

The genesis of high-performance entrepreneurship is often in sensing a larger opportunity, tucked within which could be an inventive thought. I feel that it becomes more important to sense that larger opportunity, a big picture of sorts, and have a sense of affection for what one sees as the outcome. This, followed up with hard work, results in building great businesses. Take the example of V.G. Siddhartha.

Siddhartha's family comes from Chikmagalur in Karnataka, and has grown coffee for generations. Siddhartha studied commerce in Bangalore and while doing his Masters in Mysore, left his studies midway and took a bus to Mumbai. There, in a departure from the family occupation of growing coffee, he started trading in stocks and made money, and got drawn to the world of investment in a big way. Eventually, he returned to the family business but was not happy with the size of their ambition. He wanted to make it really big. Over the years, the cultivation grew from a few hundred acres to 10,000 acres! The reason for the growth was partly driven by his desire to increase the cultivation, but in part it was because traditional growers were getting fed up with the fickle coffee prices. Many coffee estates were up for sale. As with any other agricultural crop, coffee-growing is a lot of hard work. The coffee requires year-round care: you raise it from a seedling to a berry-bearing shrub. You keep the pests at bay. You irrigate the plants only when it is needed, and to exactly the right extent. You shade them and keep wild animals at bay. Finally, after the crop is harvested, you get to know that the international coffee market has a glut and no one wants to buy your coffee even at the cost price. The cycle became so unpredictable that many growers just gave up.

Estate after estate started closing down. An El Niño, thousands of miles away, could decide a coffee grower's future in India. Siddhartha started buying up coffee estates that were going out of business.

At the same time, Siddhartha was feeling helpless—how do you carry on with a business in which you have absolutely no say regarding pricing? When he looked at the basics of the coffee business, the numbers threw him off. The world grows about 120 million bags of coffee every year. The price of that crop is approximately $7 billion. But when the same bean is retailed and becomes coffee in your cup, the value becomes $100 billion! The grower cannot determine his price, but the one selling you a cup of coffee certainly does. Everyone who buys the bean invariably negotiates with the grower, but nobody ever has gone and haggled over the price of a cup of coffee anywhere in the world. You pay whatever the person at the counter asks for.

Siddhartha thought to himself that instead of moaning about El Niño and international coffee cartels, the thing to do was to chase the $100 billion opportunity and not the $7 billion problem. He called in his advertising agency and they heard him out, but cautioned him against retailing coffee. They said, and rightly so, that the coffee market was growing at a mere 2 per cent annually. The mom and dad and two kids in a south Indian home were actually even reducing their coffee intake. To Siddhartha, however, that was not the market.

He wanted young boys and girls in cities and towns, college-going teenagers, to drink his brew. He wanted them to come and hang out in bright, fun places where they could drink their choice of coffee, watch music videos, snack on a piece of cake or a sandwich, and check their e-mail. In 1993, Café Coffee Day was born to the tagline 'A lot can happen over a cup of coffee'. Today, the Café Coffee Day chain has 302 outlets in sixty-five cities and towns all over India. While coffee-drinking in homes was either coming down or stagnating, Siddhartha saw coffee becoming a 'lifestyle' drink. More than just the brew went into the creation of the Café Coffee Day enterprise. It is what I call big-picture thinking.

While on the topic of looking at the big picture to anticipate a certain trend, and sensing an opportunity within that, I am reminded of my visit to a Toto plant in Japan. For those of you who do not know, Toto is one of the most respected manufacturers of sanitary fittings in the world. It was some time in 1996 that I visited this leader in total quality management. Toto was explaining to us their concept of 'anticipative management', which helps them give shape to new product ideas. At the time, Toto was working on a whole new range of ceramic products designed for elderly people, because Toto had figured out that by the turn of the century, 25 per cent of the Japanese population would be moving over to the other side of sixty-five, and an increasingly higher number of the Japanese population would begin greying. This, they foresaw, would create a demand for products and services that would help in the overall area of 'assisted living'. The move is illustrative of what Peter

Drucker, the legendary management philosopher, said before he died in 2006—people do not know how profound the impact of demographic changes in the world will be in the twenty-first century, and how that will bring in unusual opportunities and dislocations for the world of business. Toto had anticipated that years before.

Captain Gorur R. Gopinath, a graduate from the prestigious National Defence Academy, joined the Indian Army in the aviation branch. After serving for some years, he took voluntary retirement and returned to Bangalore. He decided to go in for organic farming in his village, where he had some family-owned land that had become more or less a wasteland. He decided to regenerate the place, and started growing fruits and vegetables there. As his daughter grew up and began her schooling in Bangalore, he had to split time between Bangalore and his farm in Javagal. During that period, whenever he visited Bangalore, he would take time off for a round of squash with one of his old buddies who used to fly helicopters in the army. One day, his friend told him that he had accepted the job of a regional manager with a courier company. That hit Gopinath really hard—what would a career helicopter pilot do in a courier company? Why should it come to this? The thought bothered him for a long time. During this time, he took a group of farmers to visit China. Along the way, he read the story of a woman from Vietnam. She had run away to France from her bomb-ravaged country as a child. As an immigrant, she grew up there to become a helicopter pilot. After everything settled down, as a grown-up, she visited Vietnam and her heart broke to see the state of her country. She remained in

Vietnam and started a helicopter service there because she felt that unless the country was made accessible, development would be difficult. The infrastructure simply did not exist for any other mode of transport.

That made sense to Gopinath. He felt that the concept was applicable to India, where infrastructure remains poor and many parts are quite inaccessible. 'We have not been bombed, but our infrastructure is as bad,' he told himself. Airports were few and far between, and the quality of roads overall quite poor. And his buddies who had flown helicopters all their lives were ending up as managers in courier companies, or taking up positions in administration and security in corporate organizations.

Gorur Gopinath says, 'Decisions are often taken before they are made.' He returned from his trip overseas, raised just about enough money, and started a helicopter charter company in 1995. Deccan Aviation was born with a single helicopter. Gopinath recruited a few ex-army pilot colleagues, and as a collegial adventure, the group began flying from a rundown airstrip in Jakkur, near Bangalore. The service caught on, the clients consisting mostly of businessmen visiting India and politicians, during their infamously frequent election campaigns. The real brainwave was yet to come. It came one day as his helicopter was flying from Bangalore to Goa. For some reason, he told the pilot to fly low so he could see the ground below more clearly.

What he saw changed everything. As the helicopter flew over vast stretches of land, hamlet after hamlet appeared and went away. Some had tiled roofs, some had thatched tops. But in every hamlet, Gopinath saw a television antenna on the rooftop and in some, he even saw a dish antenna. In that instant, his mind unfolded a new picture of India. It was an India, 'not of a billion hungry mouths to be fed, but a billion hungry customers whose needs must be satisfied'. Air Deccan was born as an idea in his mind.

In India, before the influx of budget airlines, air travel was a luxury. Most people preferred to travel by train despite the attendant inconveniences. It occurred to Gopinath that if he could take advantage of the huge population of India and run a no-frills, low-cost airline, it would be a good alternative to travelling by train. In fact, his motto became 'one billion opportunities', an allusion to the one billion population of India. He said to himself that by driving costs down, he would give every Indian at least one chance to fly in his or her lifetime. Air Deccan was born out of the larger realization that the ordinary Indian needed to fly! Today, Gopinath has more than forty-seven aircraft and helicopters that do 260 take-offs and landings a day in fifty-six airports—making Air Deccan a contender for the no. 1 position in terms of flight operations. In 2005, they flew 3 million passengers and in 2006, that number will touch 8 million!

If Siddhartha and Gopinath created sizable businesses by working in a future-backward manner, the next great story of high-performance entrepreneurship is one that, in its formative years, was built in a present-forward manner.

Leslie Auchincloss, an Irishman who had business interests in the world of enzymes, was interested in developing papain, an enzyme derived from papaya. He wanted to set up a business in India but did not know anyone who could be a good partner. An Australian brewer named Colin Dowzer had an idea. There was this brilliant young woman who had trained under him and had since returned to India. Why not speak to her, he told Colin.

At 25, Kiran Mazumdar was nursing her 'disappointment and disillusionment'.

She was the daughter of a brewer who had worked all his life for someone else, barring an aborted venture to help his nephew with a business in Gujarat. He had raised her as an independent-minded girl at a time when working women took to more middle-of-the-road professions like teaching, medicine and engineering. Kiran decided to go to Australia to study brewing instead, and returned to become quite the exception in a male-dominated industry. As India's first woman master-brewer, she did not find a job. That is when she met Leslie. Kiran heard him out and said three things: 'I am a woman, I have never done any business and I have no money.' Leslie persisted, and more as a compromise, Kiran decided to give it a try—it was the best way for her to play a significant role in an industry where no one was willing to accept her on her terms. From what she wanted to be started the process of what she was meant to be. A company was incorporated.

That was Biocon, started as a quirky idea in 1978.

Kiran went off to Ireland, learnt about how enzymes are made, and returned to make papain in India. But her destiny did not lie in making papain for the rest of her life. She felt that her true calling was 'research'. She wanted to research the creation of newer enzymes. Business boomed. She went back to her collaborators and asked them to tell her about areas on which they had not focused. They told her to research alternatives to a lot of enzymes which they had to buy from Japan. She developed processes through which the microbial enzymes could be made in India. But in all this, what did the present hold for her? The worldwide enzyme business was just about $1billion in size. It was too small a pond to fulfil her growth needs.

She asked herself, where is the next great opportunity? The world of biopharmaceuticals seemed to be a likely prospect. She felt that the basic technology behind both enzymes and biopharmaceuticals was the same. Both dealt with protein technology. The regulatory hurdles in the latter were high, but so what. Kiran got into insulin and then into antibodies. During all this, she also started the business of clinical research. She saw opportunities galore in the numbers that made up the Indian population. India was fast emerging as the diabetes headquarters of the world, with one in every five a diabetes candidate. She saw huge potential in drug testing for international pharmaceutical companies because of the incidence of disease and the diversity of India's population. From nothing in 1978, Biocon crossed revenues of $175 million in 2006, reaching a staff strength of about 2000 scientists, technicians and other highly competent workers.

How does Kiran Mazumdar-Shaw choose one idea over another? She asks herself seven questions. Do I have a basic understanding of the area? Do I know something about what is happening in the larger space of that idea? How will I build differentiation, particularly if the idea is a common product? How do I make it affordable and at the same time, deliver high value? Wherever there is a collaborator involved in the ideation process, how do I create larger leverage through the relationship beyond just that one idea? Do I know upfront who will be a paying customer and how I will go about marketing my idea? Finally, do I have conviction about the idea? Because without conviction, sooner or later, there will be the naysayer who will tell the world that it isn't such a good idea after all.

*

So how do all these people spot opportunities? They look at the big picture, they see where the world around them is going and within that framework they see connections between their innate capabilities, emergent needs and the challenge of building an organization. That process is less a step and more a staircase.

The other interesting thing about these people is that they are passionate about the line of business they have chosen. Siddhartha loves the coffee business, Gopinath loves flying and Kiran has always liked the world of brewing and enzymes and biopharmaceuticals. These people are wide-eyed and inquisitive: they are full of questions and in love with life.

Shifting the conversation to you, the question is, as you pursue your dreams, what does the writing on the wall tell you? Low-cost housing? Micro-credit? Retail? Water? Security? Hospices? Leisure travel? Education? Energy-efficient vehicles? Content creation and management? Music and entertainment? Counselling? Garbage recycling? Tree-grooming services? Pet food?

Which of these is the world going to need for a long time? Which of these could you use to make life simpler for many people? Which of these do you love?

The germination of an idea behind an enterprise often happens in solitude and contemplation. It need not require thumbing through fat feasibility reports that a bunch of MBAs have written—if they have figured it all out, why aren't they already in the business?

It helps to see the world around you, and to think of the way things might change in the next decade or two, and chances are that in thinking backwards from the future, your great idea will emerge.

Sometimes the idea is neither original nor earth-shaking, but the execution had better be, and that changes the name of the game. That is what the Apple iPod is all about. All the technologies that have gone into it were known to not one, not a dozen, but hundreds of companies from Taiwan to the US for years. Yet, it was the way in which Apple went about it that changed the rules of the game.

If you ever visit the Narayana Hrudayalaya in Bangalore, a super-speciality heart and neuro-surgery hospital set up by Dr Devi Shetty, you will realize what I mean. Dr Devi Shetty's state-of-the-art hospital is a place of pilgrimage for many: patients, their relatives, medical experts, policy makers and students of innovation. When you enter the hospital, you see two receptions. One is for Bengali-speaking people, and the other is for everybody else. Why? Dr Devi Shetty attracts a huge number of Bengali-speaking patients and their relatives from West Bengal as well as Bangladesh. To him, healing begins with communication. It is that simple.

Why is it that other healthcare providers do not get it?

Today, Dr Devi Shetty is contemplating a 5000-bed health city right next to his hospital for people from all over the world, specially the Arab world, as people there are facing increasing difficulty in getting US visas to get expensive healthcare needs fulfilled.

Sometimes entrepreneurs get their ideas while visiting tradeshows or attending industry events, sometimes while networking with other entrepreneurs and venture capitalists, sometimes by reading up reports on global trends, sometimes by visiting research institutions, sometimes by simply asking why and often, why not.

The outcome may be complex technology and breakthrough design. The outcome could be utterly, intuitively simple like the dial on the iPod or the saree-clad, Bengali-speaking lady at the reception counter in Narayana Hrudayalaya. Common to both these examples is an idea that solves the problems of a lot of ordinary people, in a simple way. Such ideas evolve naturally into high-performance entrepreneurship.

FOUR

Choosing the Team

It was August 1993. I had just returned to India after a
very successful stint in the US during which I was entrusted
with setting up the base for Wipro's International Technology
Division (ITD) in Silicon Valley. The ITD had been created
as the business arm of Wipro's R&D and worked as a cost
centre designing computers for the Indian market. This was
the time the winds of economic liberalization began to blow
in India. As scores of international computer companies
opened shop in India, it was clear that the days of
domestically focused R&D were over. However, instead of
shutting it down, the decision was to utilize it as a global
'lab-on-hire'.

I was sent to Silicon Valley to get business from
companies like Intel, Sun, Novell and Tandem. The
experience had transformed me in many fundamental ways.
On the downside, however, my tolerance for organizational
inefficiencies had come down. In the Valley, you learn to
develop affection for speed and professionalism. In twenty-
four hours, you could incorporate a company in the US. An

overnight delivery meant an overnight delivery. Living in the US, you became used to a highly customer-oriented, efficiency-seeking system. In 1993, three years after getting the operation off the ground, I returned to India. Once back, I often felt restless with the system. The speed at which it worked, in many ways, was not what I was used to. It got tested one day when a loan application was mishandled by the Human Resource (HR) department.

I was very upset with the HR folks who had first sat on my application and then made a calculation error, delaying the entire thing beyond my tolerance level. I needed the money urgently as I wanted to pay the deposit for a house I wanted to buy. I demanded that the person concerned come and meet me—I wanted to give him a dressing down. The word went out that I was very upset. Soon the staffer appeared in my room, escorted by a lanky young MBA who had just joined the company's HR team. I was a little surprised because he had nothing to do with the loan application process and it irritated me that he had also come along.

He stood there, shielding the junior person who was actually responsible, and kept telling me he was sorry that the matter had been mishandled and that he would take personal responsibility to set it right. Since I had rehearsed the admonishment, I proceeded to lash out at the duo in any case. The two stood there for the five minutes of fuming and after I had vented my feelings, the young man again apologized to me and repeated that he would get back and take personal responsibility to set things right. The two left the room.

I watched them walk back and wondered what the young MBA was made of! Why did he have to come to get rebuked by me for something he had not done? Why did he have to withstand my five minutes of dressing down? Why did he not interrupt me even once during my outburst? He let me speak and used his patience to calm my anger—all the while protecting his colleague. He owned up the entire transaction!

As he left, I told myself that some day if I were to start a company on my own, this one had to be picked up. Tadipati Gurucharan Prasad was all of twenty-three years old at that time. After a stint in Wipro, changing tracks from HR to sales, he left for Singapore, returned to India and started a new assignment implementing SAP for PricewaterhouseCoopers' clients in India. I had kept track of him meanwhile and when we started MindTree in 1999, I asked him over to set up our HR department. Under his leadership, MindTree's People Function (as we call our HR) became one of the most admired in India as the company's staff strength rapidly grew from zero to more than a thousand in the first five years. Like Prasad, I personally knew each of the initial seed team in a deep professional sense. I had seen them in moments of adversity and through their responses to these got to know their character. I always admired them professionally before liking them personally. It is very interesting, however, that socially, we were never very intimate. We knew each other's families but seldom met outside of work—we did not drink beer together or go on holidays. While compatibility is important, personal liking and social contact is of secondary consideration while building a professional team. Sometimes, we seek sameness when what we are actually looking for is complementarity.

When I was leaving Wipro after a decade of working there, Azim Premji called me in in one last bid to talk me out of my decision. As we sat in his sparsely decorated office overlooking Bangalore's busy MG Road, he asked me why I wanted to leave. I had thought through the answer beforehand. 'We are two very different people, Mr Premji,' I heard myself say. He remained silent for a couple of seconds and replied with his signature simplicity, 'That is the precise reason we should be working together.'

Though I left Wipro, I took those words with me. When you build a team, you do not start by looking at compatibility and sameness. You look for complementary skills and diversity.

MindTree's gestation period was a long fourteen months. During that time, the start-up team was put together across two continents. All through the process, we were very clear in our minds as to who was going to bring what to the table, and who would do what after the company became operational.

In any start-up team, there are a few things that the founding team must possess from day one, whatever may be the business idea. These include the ability to bring business, the ability to produce and deliver, the ability to read numbers and the ability to negotiate with investors. These qualities must be innate in the starting team. This is not to mean that the founders should go on to handle functions in sales, delivery and finance all by themselves. At a certain stage, and sooner rather than later, other professionals must be brought in who will handle these functions on a full-time basis. But there is absolutely no substitute to having these competencies within the start-up team. Because, one day, you have to get the first sale, deliver the first product and negotiate with the real estate developer, the bank and the suppliers, besides the people who will bring in investment.

If the founders themselves do not possess these capabilities, they need to co-opt someone who does on a full-time basis, and make the seed team complete. I have seen many instances of entrepreneurs either not letting go or valuing intimacy over competency in the early stages of the enterprise. Many opt to go to a relative or to a friend who promises to help 'on a part-time basis'. The story goes like this. My wife's brother is working as an accountant who will help us on a part-time basis. Or, my friend works with AT&T in Atlanta. He has great contacts and he will bring in the orders while we will set up the delivery infrastructure in India. These are tell-tale signs of trying to drive a car with three wheels with hope substituting for the fourth. What if the wife's brother gets laid off? Or the friend comes under unanticipated work pressure and does not succeed in getting you the orders? How much would you figure in their global priorities?

Friends are meant to give you good wishes, pray for you, occasionally bail you out with a personal loan, and show up in the days leading up to the IPO to make a small investment. They are not meant to pound the streets for you. You have to build your own team to do that and you have to do it yourself. Likewise, you must be able to create a spreadsheet, make sense of a cash flow statement and be able to question the basis of any financial deal.

When I look at great founding teams, I invariably see

nine characteristics. When you set up your very own 'A' team, look for these. If you find any of the elements missing in it, you would do well to rethink the team composition.

1. Proven competence, ability to pull one's weight

As you begin thinking about the core team, carefully look for people who have proven competence, not just the capability to impress you in a preliminary interview. I come across a lot of people who claim to have written many papers, spoken at many conferences, filed patents in a large corporate set-up and so on. But look at them closely and you will find someone who has been a product of his or her environment. Not someone who has created the environment—however small it might have been.

You will find a lot of cerebral people who have never led a team through corporate rough waters or pulled their organization out of difficult customer situations. They are unlikely to be effective as a seed team in building a company ground-up.

The other absolutely critical aspect of choosing a team is to look for the ability to pull one's weight, in fact the weight of a few others too. If someone does not have it in him or is not willing to do it, he has no place in the set-up. A start-up is no place for overheads. People must be able to earn their own upkeep and some more. Every individual must be closely associated with the business-creation process. Either you bring business or you execute business. Alongside there may be a few people who assist those who do either of the two and their presence is justified only when their value addition is direct, visible and measurable. Everyone else is an overhead.

Often, you will be tempted to consider a very well known person who has just retired. He may tell you that he has great ideas and contacts and he will open doors for you while sitting at home. Beware, this is not a person who will ever have skin in the game—he will not lose sleep when your sales are drying up. Building a company is not a part-time engagement.

2. Complementary Composition

MindTree is a great example of complementary composition. I am supposedly good at long-term thinking, marketing and people development and that kind of stuff. Krishna Kumar combines the capability to sell, read numbers and intuitively understand technology issues. Parthasarathy is good at setting up and leading large delivery teams, rolling out processes and handling customers. Rostow Ravanan is good at working with numbers, negotiating with financial institutions, working with complex deals. Scott Staples is good at selling high-value, consulting-led assignments; he is also good at numbers and works well with delivery teams. Anjan Lahiri is good at wowing customers with his consulting capability, facilitation skills and ability to question strategy. Kamran Ozair brought with him a deep understanding of technology, and an ability to architect large systems and lead customer-facing delivery teams. Srinivasan Janakiraman is good at understanding technology trends at a systems level, setting up and managing large R&D teams and reading numbers. Kalyan Banerjee is good at technology and managing R&D people as well as leadership development. Finally, Ashok Soota brings the unmatched capability to inspire confidence, manage investors, build consensus in teams and help them to win large deals.

This is a team that can be airdropped on an uninhabited island and it will fend for itself. As the organization grew, the same complementary composition became a way of organization building for us. Even more competent people came on board to grow MindTree—many with competencies ahead of what the founders brought. That is how a great company is created.

But, all that comes only later. To begin with, you need a team whose members make up for each other's weaknesses and occasional failings, a team that looks like an organization in microcosm. When you are able to do that, you have two great things going for you: the ability to attract investors on fair terms and the ability to attract the subsequent talent. When the core is strong, it becomes easier to attract other good people around it. This is what I call the fractal geometry of organization building.

3. Multitasking capability

A start-up organization requires the seed team to have built-in capability to do more than what the individual members are responsible for. In addition to doing one's identified task, at any time people should have the capability to step into each other's shoes. As time goes by, events unfold, exigencies happen. When the seed team demonstrates dynamic configurability, it inspires confidence within and outside.

Vikram Seth writes in one of his poems, 'Departure Lounge', 'Long distance runners learn to bear/Segmented pain'. The words are very true for people who come together to start an organization. Read carefully, they unfold the essence of building a great organization. One, it is not a sprint, it is invariably a marathon—one that never ends. Two, as in a marathon, in different legs of the journey, you will experience different kinds of pain. Three, you absolutely must budget for those so that you are not surprised by the inevitable.

In the early years, you may win a great piece of business from a new marquee customer. However, the customer may require that a senior person be co-located at their site to give them the necessary comfort and insist that only one of you would do. Faced with a situation like that, do you move the person or do you dither? Or, think of a situation that is less fortunate—a co-founder has a fractured leg and will remain in a cast for three months or a key employee has just quit. In all such exigencies, it is important to keep the momentum without missing a beat. This requires phenomenal ability and willingness to multitask. As an organization matures, it is necessary to retain that spirit so that every senior person becomes responsible for at least one additional organization-wide key responsibility. Every senior person is charged with oversight for a major account. It not only reduces the risk of turbulence, it creates stretch and accountability in senior members of the team and involves everyone in winning business and delivering it.

4. Shared Vision

The word vision as defined by the dictionary means the act or faculty of seeing, but also a thing or idea perceived vividly in the imagination, a view of something that does not yet exist. Joel Barker, a futurologist, says that it is the primary job of leaders to create the vision. Because, leaders are people who others 'opt to follow to a place they would not go by themselves'. Thus, leaders must have the vision of that place, a place that invariably sits across a chasm. It is they who must sell the vision to build a community around it and take it to its fulfilment. Vision, Barker says, must be measurable and timebound. It is something that must be uplifting and inspirational because people rally around calls to climb mountains, not molehills. In fact Barker's film *The Power of Vision* is a must see (see Entrepreneurship Resources at the end of the book) for entrepreneurs who want to build something memorable.

Sometimes, when teams come together, they often do so because of reasons other than a shared vision. In fact, if you were to put teams through a structured 'visioning exercise' in which each individual articulates why he or she is there, you would find enormous variations in what each one thinks the goal is, their personal expectations from it and commitment towards it.

Rarely do teams come together and consciously articulate a shared understanding of the future they want to create and want to be part of. Sometimes, it is serendipity that brings teams together and as they journey, events force them to ask, 'Why are we doing what we are doing?'

Articulating a shared vision is critical for the continuance of the organization. Someone may say, 'I want to build a great company that will be a leader in its field.' Someone else may say, 'I want to personally get my first million in five years and retire thereafter.' Both are legitimate visions of a future, though not compatible ones. The first requirement of a great team is individual competence. Thereafter the glue is the shared vision. A shared vision is the sketch, the artist's impression of a future in which the team would live.

5. Transparency

Some of the founders at MindTree knew each other very well, even before we thought of starting MindTree. Yet, during our very first, formal session, we took up the issue of transparency and governance. We talked about what these words meant to each one of us and discussed what would be the common acceptable framework within which we would create the organization. I distinctly remember the day we sat around in a circle in a meeting room at the Park Hotel in Vishakhapatnam, to discuss personal backgrounds, our needs, desires, fears, anxieties and even our medical histories. Each one took turn to share any and all information that could potentially impact the unborn organization. That day, we learnt more about each other than what the years of working together had taught us.

While every individual has a private side to him and is entitled to his privacy, any aspect that can affect the working of the person or impact the collective future must remain in a shared domain. Not only that, such information has to remain current at all times so that no one is taken by surprise. It is through this initial exercise that we instilled transparency at the founding team level. As the organization gets built, the value of transparency has to extend to the smallest of personal dealings. For example, each time a spouse accompanies any of us on an official tour, even though she pays for her ticket and her share of any expense, we ensure that Ashok is pre-informed about it. When one of us receives a memento or a gift or an honorarium, it is promptly notified. We continue to inform each other whenever a medical condition is reported that may remotely affect our work in the future. Founders do not bring in blood relatives to work for MindTree, nor can such people have a beneficial business relationship with MindTree. Some of these conditions may seem unreasonable at first glance, but in them lies the foundation of an open, trusting and politics-free organization.

6. Personal integrity and mutual trust

What is integrity? It is difficult to define the term. Synonyms include honesty, veracity, truthfulness, honour and uprightness. The antonym grabs you in an instant—it is dishonesty. People who come together to build an organization must have the highest confidence in each other's personal integrity and be sure that trustworthiness is not an issue. Nor is it prudent to take on someone just because it may give business a boost. Sometimes a would-be investor brings in someone and just because the investor is making a recommendation, you feel you do not have to do your own due diligence, or feel obligated to take the person in, waiving a probe into his or her values. Such a personal policy is a fairly common reason for the failure of start-up organizations.

At MindTree, as I look back at each of the ten co-founders and think of their integrity and trustworthiness, a simple test comes to my mind. If, for some reason, I am not around tomorrow, could I trust my children's affairs with any of these men? The answer is a big 'yes'. That dependability is founded on the total confidence in their integrity and trustworthiness in all inter-personal dealings. As I said before, there is always the temptation to settle for the 'rainmaking' capability of an individual—whether it is to help get immediate business or source early funding. 'Let me take this man,' I tell myself. 'So, what if his dealings are a trifle shady? He is sure to bring in some quick business. Later on, we can always figure out a way if things do not work out.' That line of thinking is tactical and may even work in good times. If a potential team member lacks integrity, however competent the person may be, he or she poses an institutional risk. Integrity is not a matter of convenience and partitioning. In my opinion, someone who lacks integrity in personal transactions cannot be depended upon in a professional sense as you build an organization. In building an organization, the lines separating the personal and the professional get blurred.

In tough times, what plugs the leaking dyke are personal integrity and trust. Each person must have the same standards about what is expedient and what is right.

The standards of personal integrity and trustworthiness of the seed team will determine the shared understanding of organizational integrity and corporate governance at a later date. In a murky business environment, organizations that stand for integrity are immediately differentiated. They attract premium valuation because a potential investor knows the risk of giving money to someone who will cut corners. High-integrity organizations attract customers who are looking for long-term engagement and employees as well. More than ever before, people are extremely networked in today's day and age. Before accepting a job offer, people check references and feel more comfortable working with clean organizations.

As you build the organization, it will become important to widely communicate a formal integrity policy. It must be communicated to everyone who comes on board so that a shared understanding is developed about what integrity means and how far would the organization go to protect it. Apart from building the shared understanding, it is also necessary to build a social memory of how the organization actually dealt with issues involving either interpretation or moments of truth when breach of integrity occurred. At MindTree, we publish these in book form. It is called *All About Integrity* and the book is given away to our competitors, suppliers and educational institutions for wider dissemination.

7. Ability to question each other and take disagreement in stride

The freedom to disagree is sometimes more important than the ability to agree.

If teammates are not capable of thinking on their own and thinking together, they cannot build a great organization. Thinking together does not mean thinking alike. Thinking on their own would mean that sometimes team members must disagree with each other. That is a good thing. What is not a good thing is confusing issue-based disagreement with personal disagreement. Good teams do not confuse the two. I met a group of three outstanding technical managers-turned-entrepreneurs. They built a great team and today run a fairly successful start-up. It is small but profitable and they build their own intellectual property and license it to mostly telecommunications companies. The three managers became close friends and that is how they built the company. As close friends, they used to agree on most things—that is how friendship is built. But once the company got off to a start, they started disagreeing on certain issues. More than the content of disagreement, they started worrying that their arguments could damage their friendship and because the line between friendship and professional fellowship was blurred, every act of disagreement got interpreted as an affront. It took a while for them to realize that while in friendship, agreement is essential, in business, disagreement may be more beneficial to the enterprise. But what becomes critical is building the maturity to be able to deal with disagreements and harvest great decisions by making it a process.

Diversity of thinking and constructive confrontation bring out the best in teams. They also involve each person's ability to see things from a unique vantage point. Yet, great teams know when to stop arguing and where to draw the line. In MindTree, we disagree on issues routinely but when we walk out of the room, we go out with a single plan of action. Personal ego is subordinate to an organization's progress. The important thing about disagreements is the self-confidence, mutual trust and candour to voice them. If people were to hesitate to say what they genuinely feel, it would be difficult to build a great organization together.

When a core team is able to practise and present diversity in thinking, it spreads to the rest of the organization. In such an organization, people speak up rather than keep things inside because they know that this is a way of getting to the best decisions. Azim Premji used to often tell his team: 'Do not walk around with constipation.' It is sensible advice: keeping things bottled up can ultimately create a stink.

8. Resilience

As you build a company, things never go exactly as per plan. On the way, start-up teams suffer high highs and low lows. More than once in the first few years of existence, every entrepreneur will go through feelings of helplessness, rejection and loss of direction.

Key people leave at a time you least expect them to.

Assured business just goes away.

A competitor pulls the rug from under your feet with a discontinuous business model.

Your board or your venture capitalist or your partner behaves in a strange manner. Sometimes, they choose to do so at the same time.

How does one deal with such unscripted situations? In addition to such possibilities, we actually live in times when there is a high probability that a 'low probability' event will happen. Who knew 9/11 would happen? Who knows when the next pandemic will hit the world? Who knows when and how the avian flu virus will mutate? You do not know; all you know is that you have to be resilient.

Resilience—it is that one thing above everything else, that makes entrepreneurs very different from everyone else. Take resilience out and you just cannot become an entrepreneur. Sometimes, I feel, it is not the greatness of an idea or an individual but the sheer ability to hang on that helps create great organizations. It comes from within the entrepreneur. If you are able to hold on to the reef for the night, tomorrow is another day. While you are holding on, many people will drop by with advice.

Three months into the life of your organization and thereafter at least twice every year a passer-by—usually a Wall Street animal or a completely uninformed but well-dressed analyst—will come by and tell you about the futility of your size. He will cite a Gartner or an IDG or a McKinsey research that has all but conclusively proven why companies like yours must sell off or just wither away. Sometimes, you may even see the signs of that happening in the market around you. 'Look,' they may say, 'company X could not scale and had to be sold. Only at the size that companies Y and Z have, do you get large chunks of repeatable business. How will you ever get there?' Or, consider this: 'Just see the plans Company A has. Look at the resources at their command—they will just come, raise salaries by 100 per cent and hire by the thousands, your people will just leave in droves.' There is a nice story that I know about the power of resilience—of listening to the voice within and sometimes doing the intuitive thing.

When IBM returned to India in 1990, after banishment for decades, they chose Bangalore as their headquarters. Wipro was not even a $100 million company. The first thing to happen was that several key managers, impressed with the IBM name and a fat salary increase, left. Azim Premji was told by many to sell off his computer hardware business. How could his company survive the muscle of an IBM? To add to that, there were Compaq, Digital and HP knocking at the door. The most telling signal in favour of giving in was something that happened overnight. The expatriate country manager at IBM persuaded the landlord of Wipro's 88 MG Road office to let him put up the IBM neon sign on top of the building that housed the entire Wipro IT group top management. When it lit up, people thought Wipro would just become a shadow of the past. Azim Premji did not have the answers, but he just hung in there. Today, the neon sign does not exist and Wipro has not given up the tenancy of that otherwise nondescript building, which still houses some functions. But every visiting CEO and state head who comes to Bangalore does make Wipro's sprawling campus a few miles away a must stop.

Resilience is not just about professional issues that may come and go. While you are trying to build a company by breathing and dreaming your vision, you may have problems with a loved one at home, or you may run into a serious health issue that needs addressing. The most memorable account of resilience in the face of personal adversity that I have come across in recent times is that of champion biker Lance Armstrong. His is a story of grit and determination in the face of unmatched adversity as he battled with multiple cancer in the prime of his youth and his biking career. His account of the struggle and his victory can be found in a book titled *It's Not About the Bike: My Journey Back to Life.*

9. Sense of humour

Humour is, indeed, a very serious issue. People who cannot laugh at a situation or at themselves, cannot pull their enterprise over the long haul. Sometimes, it is the ability to laugh at trivial things and the ability to laugh with each other. Sometimes, it is the ability to laugh after the roof has just blown away. While organization building is a serious affair, a sense of humour makes it a bearable experience.

If a person is highly competent but lacks a sense of humour, I would not take such a person as part of a seed team. That person is welcome to move in after the house is built.

Successful teams are like tribes in their own right. They show the same bonding that comes from many things. Among them are their favourite jokes and pranks and comedy scripts in which they star. It is a great way to decompress and gives people the capability to see the brighter side of things. Often they are like high-school pranksters and that is what brings out their creative side.

Even after many years at MindTree, there are times when we have a serious and possibly heated debate inside a conference room. We take strong positions against each other. But the moment we step out, it is as if nothing had happened and we do silly things and laugh at each other.

FIVE

DNA, Mission, Vision and Values

It was the spring of 1999. I was sitting with Shombit Sengupta, founder of Shining Strategic Design, in his studio in Paris one evening prior to starting MindTree. Shombit is internationally acclaimed for his work in strategic branding.

Strategic branding relates to the creation of a corporate identity and communication of the brand. It is part management and part witchcraft. What makes the world adore the Nike swoosh? Why is the classic Coca-Cola bottle shaped the way it is? How do service organizations like banks, hotels and software companies convey the essence of their brands to prospective customers, investors and employees? They hire a brand consultant and probably, later on, an advertising agency to bring out the brand proposition in a visual manner. People like Shombit are able to get into the strategic aspects of a brand. They look at the essence of the corporate personality, study how the market perceives the organization and based on a deep understanding of the true value an organization produces as well as its aspirations, suggest the overall brand strategy. Shombit and I have known each other for quite some time. We first met when Azim Premji brought him in, to redo Wipro's brand. At that time, I used to be the chairman of Wipro's Corporate Sales and Marketing Council. My job in the initial days of engagement with Shombit was to be a conduit between Shombit's ideas and the rest of the organization. Since then, I had moved to Lucent and a chance visit to Paris brought me back in the company of a man I had a lot of admiration for. One evening, when I went to see Shombit in his studio, we began talking about the future. When I told him about the desire to start a high-end IT consulting and software services company, he asked me, what would be the proposed company's DNA?

I had not thought about that. We all think of positioning and differentiation and marketing strategy. But DNA? And that too for a company? What's that? But come to think of it, every human being's uniqueness lies in his DNA. It is how we pass on something of ourselves to our progeny. Likewise, every organization that is born and will continue in time must have its own DNA. It is the reason for its existence—something that cannot be changed without changing the very structure of everything that the organization represents.

The thought deeply touched me and we talked more about it.

As a result of this conversation, the founders of MindTree got together and we settled that the DNA of MindTree would be imagination, action and joy. These three, together, would stand for who we were and who we wanted to be. Why imagination, action and joy?

Imagination, because our clients require solutions that

are new and different. Action, because we must take responsibility for what we advise our clients. It also connotes high achievement orientation. Joy, because while delivering imagination and action, we want to convey happiness—the world does not like to deal with people who do not radiate joy in what they do. Think of your favourite salesman, the mechanic you really like or the dentist who seems to be enjoying her work. We instinctively like to entrust ourselves to people who not only know their work but seem to enjoy themselves doing it.

I think the concept of a corporate DNA is very powerful. It conveys the essence of the organization to people who come on board. However, it is not just a set of nice-sounding words that you pick up from nowhere. These must be deeply thought through and the seed team must believe in them—they must resonate with them, convey to them the spirit of what they do.

The next important step is to settle the mission statement of the company. A mission statement is often called a North Star statement. It is aspirational and direction setting. It is a statement that shows what the company wants to be.

In our case, we said: We will deliver business-enabling solutions and technologies, in partnership with our customers, in a joyous environment for our people.

You will notice that the mission statement flows from the DNA—it is consistent with the elements of imagination, action and joy.

Business-enabling solutions and technologies require strong elements of imagination and action and the way the mission statement is carved, the term 'joy' just jumps out. A mission statement is by design both simple and lofty. Unless it is that way, it will not be memorable. People cannot follow what they cannot remember.

A mission statement does not change every so often. It must be crafted in a way that it remains the North Star for a very long time. It must be sufficiently broad so as not to shut off future possibilities. Note that we never used the words 'IT' or 'software' in the mission statement.

Thereby leaving a whole range of possibilities open, yet marking enough of a boundary so that we were not all over the place and lost focus. Neither customers nor employees like to deal with an unfocused organization.

Here are a few examples of what mission statements are like.

Refugees International is a leading world organization that concerns itself with the issues of human displacement due to political reasons. The organization defines its mission this way:

> Refugees International (RI) generates lifesaving humanitarian assistance and protection for displaced persons around the world and works to end the conditions that create displacement.

IBM Global Business Services has a more descriptive view of what their mission is. The first line is the essence of the mission and the rest expands the 'how-to' achieve part, which sometimes is useful though difficult for people to remember and articulate.

> At IBM Global Business Services, our mission is to engage collaboratively with our clients and tackle their most complex business problems. We will apply our business

insights to develop fresh, innovative solutions that provide real and measurable business outcomes—whether that's designing and implementing new service after sales business models, revolutionizing the business model for automotive insurance with innovative technology, or becoming one of the leading logistics providers for supply chains. We will work with our clients to identify the level of change that suits their needs and that results in actionable change and sustainable outcomes. We will bring together the best of IBM—and our business partners—to effect change and optimize business performance for our clients.

Microsoft Corporation defines its mission with a lot of simplicity and is a lot more memorable, compared to what we see in the IBM example—this is not to compare the impact of the two. What matters is what works for you best. Here is what Microsoft says:

At Microsoft, we work to help people and businesses throughout the world realize their full potential. This is our mission. Everything we do reflects this mission and the values that make it possible.

We all know Google. Google states its mission statement with great simplicity and keeps the possibilities boundless. It can be seen as aspirational and at the same time criticized by some for being too broad, too open. Again, the issue is what works is what works.

Google's mission is to organize the world's information and make it universally accessible and useful.

GE, on the other hand, does not have a mission statement per se but articulates its business philosophy each year in a letter to shareholders.

The mission statement conveys the direction in which the organization must march. Whenever there is confusion on whether or not a new opportunity is to be pursued—a new line of business to be considered, for example—the mission statement becomes the touchstone. If the new opportunity is inconsistent with the mission statement, then it is a matter of fundamental shift from the original purpose for which the organization was created. While the mission statement tells us what kind of organization we want to create, the vision statement that flows from it consists of a set of intermediate goals that define success. While choosing the set of goals, it is not unusual to consider:

— A financial goal: reaching a certain level of business and profitability and return on investment in a specified time-frame
— An admiration goal: being among the best employers in a given category or to win an industry-level award or recognition
— A goal towards social sensitivity: something that the organization would stand for.

Simply put, your DNA tell others who you are. Your mission tells them who you want to be. The vision consists of intermediate, measurable and time-bound goals that you promise to yourself and to all the stakeholders. In fact, it is the most concrete but also the most prone to periodic reassessment and change. It is usual to have three to five years as a time horizon and have the vision revisited in that frequency. In MindTree, we created a vision for 2005 and as we went along, we changed that to Vision 2007-2008. It reads:

OUR VISION FOR THE YEAR 2007-08

- To achieve $231 million in revenue
- To be among the top 10 per cent in our business in terms of profit after tax (PAT) and return on investment (ROI)
- To be one of the top 20 globally admired companies in our industry
- To give a significant portion of our PAT to support primary education

The annual business plan of the company flows from the vision and in turn, determines the allocation of resources. Individual objectives then flow out of the annual plan and people get their performance evaluation done at the end of the year, based on these objectives. So, you see how there is a cascading relationship between DNA, mission, vision and individual annual objectives.

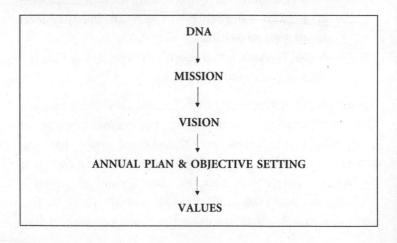

The founding team must spend all the time necessary to think these through. Yet, none of these occupy top of the mind recall of people as the organization grows. Newer people come with their way of doing things. Sometimes these complement, sometimes these add to the competence of the organization—and sometimes, these can be out of line and even destructive. This is where the organization's values come in. In order to guide the day-to-day working of everyone in the organization, it becomes critical to articulate a set of values that everyone abides by. This, over a period of time, becomes the organization's way of doing things and becomes second nature.

In MindTree, the values chosen for our day-to-day working have a set of five elements. These are: Caring, Learning, Achieving, Sharing and Social Responsibility (CLASS).

Each of these have sub-attributes. For example, Caring means caring for customers, caring for MindTree Minds, caring for our stakeholders and finally, caring for the organization. When looking for prospective MindTree Minds, particularly people at senior levels, we make it a point to determine mutual value match. In order to help people understand what each of the five elements mean, a set of explanatory attributes have been drawn up.

The CLASS values and their attributes were crafted by the first 500 MindTree Minds.

CARING

Elements	Indicative Description
Customer caring	Understands customer needs, stretches to deliver on customer satisfaction. Builds lasting bonds and trust with customers. From DNA, sees Joy as the satisfaction of a job well done.
People Caring	Sensitive to diverse cultural requirements. Displays empathy and respect for individuals. Is self-motivated and energizes fellow employees. Recognizes and respects family commitments and work-life balance.
Financial stakeholder caring	Understands the basics of business financials. Fosters cost consciousness and increased productivity. Has a resource-efficient approach in managing objectives.
Organizational Caring	Aligns team behaviour with corporate values. Refers business opportunities and industry professionals to join. Networks with business partners, industry, academia and society to enhance corporate image. Is fair in approach and creates a win-win environment with all partners. Is trustworthy and dependable.

LEARNING

Elements	Indicative Description
Development	Continuously improves on skills and knowledge. Takes responsibility for self-development and contributes to development of others through teaching and mentoring. Receptive to feedback, adapts to new environments quickly and learns effectively from unusual sources with humility.
Innovation	Champions initiatives and implements new ideas and change programs within the

organization and cross-functional teams effectively. Suggests strategic and creative solutions to problems.

ACHIEVING

Elements	Indicative Description
Aspiration	Adopts high targets and continuously raises the bar on stated goals. Possesses high energy, displays self-confidence and works hard. Has the ability to grow within the organization and take on roles of larger responsibility. Possesses drive to succeed.
Accountable	Clearly articulates vision, takes ownership for people and results. Builds high-performance teams and is driven by results. Drives quality and usage of tools as a habit. Takes pride in work and balances task completion with people orientation.
Action-Oriented	Is deadline oriented, decisive and achieves quick turnaround times. Anticipates problems and proactively works on the solutions.

SHARING

Elements	Indicative Description
Teamwork	Is a good team worker and has the ability to build teams. Takes initiative in continuous improvement plans. Helps others in difficulty and seeks help if required. Places team achievement above individual interest. Encourages openness and is approachable.
Knowledge	Creates knowledge-sharing platforms and shares knowledge effectively using existing tools.
Encouragement	Appreciates, rewards and encourages people to deliver their best.

SOCIALLY RESPONSIBLE

Elements	Indicative Description
Societal	Abides by the law of the land and other statutory regulations required.
Integrity	Maintains highest standard of integrity. Is transparent in transactions with respect to professional standards and work ethics. In case of conflict, stays with the right and not the convenient.
Commitment	Commits to corporate citizenship, drives value inculcation and institution building within MindTree.

In addition, the five CLASS values are wedded to the Performance Management System. The Performance Management System has three components against which everyone is evaluated at the end of a year. These three are: How did the person perform against the set of agreed upon annual objectives? How did the individual stack up against the competencies for a given role? And, finally, how has the person lived the CLASS values during the preceding year?

Every year, MindTree Minds evaluate their adherence to these values. The results are then reviewed by the supervisor. We also collect anecdotes that exemplify the CLASS values in action and these are propagated through the organization. Ashok Soota explains the CLASS values to each new person within the first ninety days of joining.

At MindTree, it is mandatory for people at senior levels to seek 360-degree inputs as part of the Performance Management System. The 360-degree inputs are configured around the CLASS values.

The DNA, mission, vision and values serve to create a lot of back pressure on the system. Every now and then, people question decisions and management action when they find inconsistencies. It is important for the management team to actively encourage such questioning—it is the only way to keep the system honest and send a message that the values are a shared wealth. They grow when protected by everyone in the system.

Despite the fact that the values need to be protected and nurtured, there is a strange truth about their propagation. One of the ways they get internalized is when values are violated by someone and the system watches how the management team deals with the violation. The organization's conviction gets tested when the management team has to pay a price to defend the values. We had half a dozen such situations during the first six years at MindTree when values were transgressed. Irrespective of the seniority of the person involved and the price to the business, in each case, we parted ways with the individual. These instances are documented in the book *All About Integrity* that is distributed to all MindTree Minds. In addition, the book is considered a social resource and is made available to educational institutions, competitors and anyone else who asks for it.

SIX

How Are You Different?

It is the first question any prospective investor will ask you: 'How are you different?' In a talent-starved world, every future employee will want to know how you build differentiation into what you do. If you cannot convince them, they will go to your competition. It is not just about convincing people with smart answers, though. You have to live your differentiation promise and show that it is evident at every touch point, through the products, the services and through interaction with stakeholders. After thinking through your DNA, mission, vision and values, you will have to think of a differentiation strategy. It is not an easy subject, for the simple reason that building differentiation is a very slow process. Even more interesting is the aspect of differentiation that has to do with the many intangibles at the end of the day. For instance, Apple is different because of its design, its cultish culture. Intel is different because of its ability to constantly increase microprocessor power at reduced prices. Dell is different through its knowledge of the supply chain. The Body Shop is different because of its ability to combine beauty with social activism. Jet Blue is different with its low-cost, efficient air travel concept. To each of these, differentiation is not an accident. It did not just happen by itself. In the competitive world of global business where choices outstrip demand, every stakeholder wants to know how you are different. It is not an option, it is a survival issue. The world does not look at you very kindly if your differentiation does not jump out without having to struggle with words and explanations and Power Point slides.

Many people ask me how MindTree is different. Sometimes, the people who ask that question do not really want to, or care to know the answer in a lot of depth. They are trying to test you on your cogence rather than determine how truly different you are. Only a few know enough to appreciate that differentiation is strategic, deep, embedded in process and for the most part, difficult to explain but easier to sense. It is not just the claims an organization may make, more something people gradually become aware of. A point comes when it just shows. One has to have a plan and work it every single day of enterprise building—one customer at a time and one employee at a time. There are just no short cuts here, whatever may be your line of business.

Someone said that the best way to explain the concept of differentiation is to point towards the long-haul airline business. All the airline companies buy their planes from probably either a Boeing or an Airbus. They get the engines fitted from probably one of two sources—either GE or Rolls-Royce. Similarly, they get their aircraft financed from a handful of the same companies. They all take off and land from the same airports and serve the same boring airline food. Yet, they end up being very different from each other.

So, what really makes one airline very different from another?

Why do people who fly Jet Airways or Singapore Airlines or Lufthansa know that these are very unique organizations? Capital or technology does not, in today's world, deliver differentiation. It comes from sustained management thought and practice, till it becomes the culture across, say, an organization as large as Lufthansa with its huge fleet of aircraft and pilots and staff drawn from many nationalities. How does one build that?

I have always believed that differentiation is a six-horse chariot. Six equally strong horses. They need to pull it in the same direction, at the same time, with the same energy. These six horses are: domain, tools, methodology, quality, innovation and branding.

First, let us talk about domain. Successful companies are closely associated with a primary field of focus. We cannot be everything to everyone. I cannot be great at making ice-cream and automobiles and writing great software at the same time. At least not in the beginning. Increasingly, people will choose to work with enterprises that do something so well that they are associated with that domain. In other words, they build specialization. That is how they deliver value and win customer loyalty. They are so good at the specific area of their work that people think they 'stand for it'. Focus on a domain gives the ability to stand for that something. To be world-class today, companies do not have to be large—they have to stand for something. When your enterprise stands for something, you suddenly become visible and powerful.

The world finds it easier to take note of companies that stand for something. Look at Southwest Airlines and BMI and Air Deccan—they each stand for low-cost air travel in the US, Europe and India respectively. Taj Hotels stands for great hospitality. Starbucks stands for a trendy coffee culture with environmental responsibility. Target is about affordable designs for the community, making neighbourhood retailing a relationship-driven experience. Similarly, Apple stands for innovation. Honda stands for high quality mid-range cars. Mercedes-Benz stands for luxury and flawless design. Disney stands for family entertainment. Porsche spells design and so on.

The question is, what would your company stand for? In other words, what will be your domain?

Now let us look at the second aspect of differentiation, using the right tools. Successful and differentiated companies use unique and sometimes better tools than their competitors. Ever since man has invented tools, they form a very important part of our existence. Tools help productivity. Wise and careful choice of tools decides the difference between the best and the second best. In today's world I would go even further and say that they separate the best from the second best. The difference between the two is seldom your intellect. It is usually the tools you use.

Think of the neighborhood medical centre and compare it with the best hospital in town. The difference is not just the medical talent. The difference is in the access to and the use of tools. When a patient is wheeled into the best hospital, in a matter of minutes, the doctors can use a CT scanner, do an ultrasound, a dozen tests and then zero in on the line of treatment. And it is not just today. Look at history and the role of weaponry in deciding a battle's outcome. Ibrahim Lodhi presided over India from 1517 till 1526 as the Sultan of Delhi. In 1526, his kingdom was invaded by Babur. The sultan's army far outnumbered the invaders. Babur positioned cannons in the front. The use of gunpowder in war was unknown to Lodhi's army, which had the elephants right in front. As the cannons roared, the elephants panicked, turned back and trampled Lodhi's own soldiers. It was the use of superior tools, in this case, cannons, and not the level of patriotism that decided the winner. As you grow your organization, ask yourself, what are going to be my tools? How will they be better than those used by others?

Having said that, in today's world, tools can be acquired by anyone. To stay differentiated, you have to go beyond tools and focus on the third aspect of differentiation, which is about methodology. What is methodology?

Methodology is your special way of doing things. Great enterprises lay importance on developing their way of doing things. Whenever you see a problem, before you jump in to solve it, ask yourself, what is the methodology? Have I figured it out and how can that be propagated within the organization?

People who jump into solving problems without settling the methodology may occasionally succeed. However, that success is likely to be a flash in the pan. It is not sustainable.

The power of methodology is in its ability to deliver predictable success. In life, as much as in enterprise, people like predictability. You do not want to go a doctor who is unpredictable. Would you ever fly with a pilot who is unpredictable? We seek out people who are predictable because they use solid methodology. Before you attempt the next complex problem, ask yourself, what will be my winning methodology? Once you know it, you have to refine it, evolve it and keep it sharpened. Whether it is an award-winning restaurant chain like PF Chang in the US, or a parcel delivery company like FedEx the world over, or a supply chain super-specialist like Dell or a strategy consulting firm like McKinsey—their differentiation is in the methodology that is followed like a recipe for a food preparation. They pay close attention to designing, advocating, propagating and keeping current their body of knowledge. It is an initiative driven by top management and very specialized knowledge management systems and experts are deployed to formulate the methodology, which is key to their business success.

The fourth area of focus that helps build differentiation is quality. No one wants to deal with companies that do not deliver quality products and services. The world's best companies do their work so well that they are said to run their processes at an astonishing Six Sigma level. Six Sigma is one of the ways to deploy Total Quality Management (TQM). It was conceptualized as a process at Motorola in the 1980s and then GE made it widely known as a corporate initiative under Jack Welch. Simply put, Six Sigma is a body of knowledge and practices that enable you to drive defects out of any given process or product such that you make only 3.4 mistakes—given a million opportunities! What is the essence of that level of quality? It does not happen by accident but is carefully planned and implemented. Quality-focused enterprises believe that you can deliver quality only when you begin to focus on the process rather than the end result. Process-focused enterprises are quality enterprises. Like an outstanding runner, these are people who take every aspect of their sport seriously and pay full attention to the act of delivery without getting distracted by the ribbon that is waiting to be braced at the end of the race. Organizations must have a clear quality vision, a roadmap and serious commitment at the top management level and sustain it throughout the life of the enterprise. More on that in chapter 10.

In today's competitive world, however, even quality is a given. While continuously working on it, we also have to realize the importance of focusing on innovation as a strategy to build differentiation. Innovation is the ability to continuously come up with ways and means which are *new and different*. Innovation is the ability to answer, 'What is it I do that is new and different?' If an organization cannot answer that question satisfactorily, the world does not grant it differentiation. In such a world, winners are invariably associated with their ability to think differently, act differently and deliver differently. Innovation was earlier thought of as witchcraft. Today, companies are saying, 'We want to practise innovation.' You too must ask yourself, will I follow the beaten path or will I create my own space? Being innovative is not a chance event, it is a result of the mind being trained to think in newer, more diverse and creative ways. Organizations today are spending a lot of time, energy and resources in creating an innovation-centric culture. Tools like Six Thinking Hats and TRIZ and Systems Thinking are being increasingly deployed to make people think differently. Central to the innovation process, is the role of knowledge management. More and more companies are paying attention to the use of knowledge management practices to build intellectual capital in an organization so that the end result is a steady stream of innovative processes, products and services.

Interestingly, great organizations are beginning to engage with people who have not been their traditional constituents. Think of it this way—your traditional constituent is your customer. Great companies of the world are beginning to focus on the customer's customer. If one can make a huge difference to a customer's customer, it helps build the stickiest relationship—the one with the most loyalty. To be able to do that, incremental value addition does not work. One has to be innovative. Predictable innovation begins where total quality of yesteryears ends.

Now let us look at the last area of focus for building a strategy for continued differentiation. This one is about branding. The concept comes from the cattle ranchers who brand their herds with a distinguishing mark so that they can be separated from cattle of another ranch. In modern times, the concept has become widespread as organizations use branding to establish their unique identity in the market place. It is about building mindshare among customers, suppliers, employees and investors, as well as the community at large in an increasingly connected world.

Successful, winning companies are well-branded companies. What is the essence of branding? It is not advertising as some may think. The essence of branding is in a 'value promise'. It begins with creation of innate value and through branding, that value is externalized. The world begins to see a connection between your product or service and the value they can expect to receive from it. Without great value, you cannot build a great brand. If I do not add perceptible value to my customers, employees, suppliers and investors day after day, and in some small way, even to the society around, mere advertising will only create distance between my organization and the stakeholders.

All these are the stuff that brand strategy is about and the discipline of marketing (as against sales) focuses on these. It is necessary that an expert in this area is brought on board as the organization builds momentum. The good news is that many marketing organizations as well as free-lance experts are available today who can even guide the early-state organization till the time in-house guidance becomes available to conceptualize, roll out and sustain the brand.

Now that we have talked about the six horses of differentiation, it is once again important to remind ourselves that differentiation really 'happens' when the enterprise focuses on all the six elements simultaneously. To reiterate, these are: Stand for something. Choose tools with care. Develop your own methodology. Build quality in whatever you do. Innovate—ask yourself, what is new and different today? Finally, invest in the brand.

SEVEN

Writing the Business Plan

Once the founding team has thought through the DNA, mission, vision, values and the all-too important subject of differentiation, it is time to write it all down in a document. In other words, the team is now ready for the business plan. A business plan is essentially a strategy document with particular emphasis on the fiscal aspects of the business. It drills down details to an extent that you have a three-year view of your sources of income, your investments, your expenses and the profit and loss projections.

It is amazing, though, that most people find this a very difficult exercise. There are books galore on this subject, yet many people actually drop their ideas of entrepreneurship once you tell them to go and write down a business plan. Just as you would not try to build a house without a floor plan (though, technically speaking, you could), you do not build a serious enterprise and run it year after year without a serious business plan and a business planning process in place. The business planning process, however, comes later, first you have to have a written business plan. It is not enough to enthusiastically say, 'I have a great idea.' You have to be able to say, 'I have written a great business plan and I believe in it.' That is when people begin to take you really seriously. It sounds clichéd, but you will be surprised that for every 100 people who have a great idea, only ten can convert the idea into a sensible business plan. Of these, only three truly believe in what they have written down and of them probably only one has some chance of success. While the numbers may not look encouraging, the trick is to sit down and write down that great idea as a business plan in any case. The moment you try doing that, you will discover a dozen aspects that you either did not think through or do not understand fully. This leads you to plug those holes. Without this exercise, you are not set up to succeed.

The purpose of the written business plan is to raise funding, no doubt, but it is not the primary reason. The primary reason is to create the blueprint of the house before one begins construction, even though the blueprint may keep changing as you go along. You use the essence of the blueprint to attract alliances, customers and key employees. When we started MindTree, we wrote down a fairly detailed business plan. When I read it one day, six years after, it looked MBAish to me. I was surprised by the fact that only two things quite worked out more or less the way we had anticipated. These were the topline projection in the first chapter and the elements of risks identified in the last chapter. In-between, everything changed. But even as I look back and think of the wisdom of the team, I cannot but congratulate ourselves for listing the risks accurately enough.

Most of the things we had anticipated could go wrong, actually did! That documented knowledge itself is a great benefit from the exercise.

The people who are looking at funding you know that business plans change. So, they are not necessarily worried about the details. They certainly are worried about your ability to think through issues, make a personal commitment to an overall plan, and whether you possess the flexibility and the resilience to change gears as the world around changes. They certainly assess how much you can work with numbers, how much you are able to see things in a 360-degree perspective, how well you read the market and the competitive landscape and your affinity to the planning process itself.

There are many books on the subject, as I have said before. Any financial consultant or banker can also tell you the format to use. However, in qualitative terms, the document must answer the questions below.

ISSUES TO ADDRESS AS PART OF THE BUSINESS PLAN

- What is the mission and vision of the organization?
- What is my product or service? How will it evolve as a family of products or services?
- What is the competitive landscape? How are other leading players serving the market? What trends do market research and analyst reports indicate?
- In what way will I be different? Why should someone buy my products or services?
- How will I get my first, paying customer? How will I price my goods or services?

- What will be my marketing strategy?
- What organization structure will I need? What critical skills do the founders possess and which ones need to be supplemented?
- What capital expenditure will be needed and why? How have I determined the adequacy and the cost?
- What revenue expenditure will be needed for the same period?
- How is my cost structure different from that of the competition?
- What is my three-year cash flow?
- When will the organization reach break even?
- What is the funding plan? How much of it will come from personal capital, how much from venture funding and what portion from loans?
- What is the plan for recruitment, training and retention of people?
- What are the R&D plans? How will the activity be sustained over time?
- What are the manufacturing and distribution plans?
- What are the various risks involved in building the organization?
- In what way will the team de-risk those?

As you write down the document, you should appreciate that the purpose of writing the business plan is not to impress someone into believing in your business. The purpose is to make sure that you have indeed thought through all the issues and also to uncover for yourself what you do not know. A business plan, written well, helps to attract the right talent and the right kind of investors. It becomes the basis for negotiation while attracting investment.

Remember, when you raise equity, you are in effect giving away ownership. A good business plan, written well, will set the tone for negotiating how much ownership you have to trade for how much money.

Some things in the business plan are bound to go completely awry due to unforeseen contingencies. Within a year of starting MindTree, we were hit by several successive setbacks—the Internet and the dotcom boom meltdowns and the telecom bubble-burst, 9/11 and the global economic slowdown that followed, and the SARS outbreak in Asia. Such things can never be fully anticipated and when they do happen one may have to recast the business plan. What were some of the major blows to the business because of these successive events? The viability of start-ups was questioned by large buyers; small buyers vanished from the scene altogether. Our business, being a new one, depended only on new software development. In times of severe crisis, people do not invest in new software, they only like to maintain what are called 'lights on' applications. In other words, applications without which the organization's day-to-day operations will come to a halt. There were many more such implications which were wrought by extraneous forces. More on that in chapter 14, 'Emergence and the Willingness to Change'.

When we wrote MindTree's business plan, it went through many iterations. Inevitably, as you meet different people, particularly prospective investors, you will have to refine the assumptions, your understanding of the market, alliances and competition as well as costs. It is a good idea to save the progressive versions and discuss them in detail amongst the founding team so that you are able to debug the documents as you go along. The MindTree business plan began with an executive summary. In the first chapter, we captured the business context. In this, we wrote about the broad area of our proposed operation based on the way we saw some major indicators. Thereafter, in a chapter on the company and its objectives, we narrowed the content to what would be our offerings for the kind of customers we sought to serve. In the next chapter, on core values, we elaborated upon a set of six values (these subsequently got revised after the first 500 MindTree Minds came on board), but these values were not just esoteric statements of intent. Against each core value, we explained how it would translate into customer benefits.

After that, we dwelt upon the subject of company positioning and business overview. This chapter looked at the competitive landscape and did an analysis of the major competitors globally in terms of their strengths and weaknesses and how we would be different from them. In this chapter, we further drilled down to our proposed business offerings in the areas of e-commerce and the telecom sector—areas that were on fire at that time and were identified as our sweet spot. After looking at these in depth, the next chapter was devoted to the sales and marketing strategy, a subject of great interest to venture capitalists because for a new venture, customer acquisition is key. This chapter was followed by a detailed discussion on the services and the business process delivery plan. There we focused on not just structural issues but the tools and methodologies we would invest in to create a great customer experience.

Next, we devoted a full chapter to people and organizational structure issues. This had to do with how we would expand the team, what would be the focus in training and development and how we would create a great place to work and who would do what.

Having detailed all of the above, we went on to identify the risks to the business. These ran into twenty-odd risks that spanned people, business, geo-politics, investment climate, execution and many other issues. It is amazing how many of these actually came true as we went about raising MindTree. Finally, we had the financials for the first year and the two years following. These were explained with qualitative comments giving assumptions for each entry.

The business plan you write is not going to pan out exactly the way you envision it. Having said that, it is not an airy-fairy document which is created to impress investors. It is a well-thought-out piece of strategy based on which you sign the investment term-sheet and you must believe in the contents.

The business plan is a classified document and should not be indiscriminately distributed. It is best not to forward it as an electronic copy and have a serially numbered hard copy given to anyone who must have it. You should ask for a formal non-disclosure agreement before you part with it. Any patentable idea or highly confidential data need not be shared in any great detail at the first pass and only after progressing towards some level of mutual comfort should you share it on an as-needed basis.

Let me conclude this with a story. I was actively pursuing a sales person for a role in the about to be formed MindTree.

I used to think highly of the individual and had a warm personal relationship with him. To get him on board, I went ahead and shared the business plan with him electronically. This followed a meeting with Scott Staples and Anjan Lahiri in New Jersey. Both Scott and Anjan did not think he fit the bill at that moment and for some reason, even the mutual chemistry did not match. I thought that it would be in the best interest of all concerned not to go forward with the proposal and went back to the individual to ask him to drop the idea. Justifiably, he felt spurned. But what he did next was something I had not considered. He forwarded the electronic copy of the business plan to his bosses in his current company. They considered us as a potential competitor.

Ethics and legal recourse apart, the lesson is more important—I should have been careful about distributing the business plan. Luckily, many of the things we wrote in the business plan did not quite pan out as envisioned. The document also underwent many changes at our end by the time his bosses got to read it, and the real damage was minimal. But imagine, if we were a product company! It would have been an altogether different story.

EIGHT

Choosing the Right Investor

The moment of raising capital is the moment you breathe life into the unborn child. It is a defining moment, one which will have a deep, cascading impact on many things downstream. Entrepreneurs get so caught up with first the idea of selling their dream and then the fact that someone is willing to put money into the dream, that they overlook one key dimension: the colour of the money. This chapter is about that.

In today's world, there is more money chasing a few good ideas than the other way round. So, if you truly have a good idea and a team in place that will sweat it out, there is no dearth of capital. It is therefore critical that you make a careful decision on the source of funding the venture.

There are many ways to fund your enterprise and you need to do what is right, based on your unique situation. Before you press into action, it is always a good idea to look around the experience of similarly situated entrepreneurs, network with people who are members of organizations like TiE (The Indus Entrepreneurs—www.tie.org), and talk to knowledgeable and trustworthy finance people to determine the most appropriate vehicle for funding. There are no one-size-fits-all solutions here. If you have an idea that requires full-time work for a while and you need some working capital to do it, see if you can do so from your own savings or a small loan. If it is something that requires a dozen of you to sweat it out for a year, seek an 'angel investor'—usually a wealthy private investor who gives you your first half-a-million dollars. Only later should you seek venture capital. Typically, venture capital funds come in two types—early state and late state. Early-state funds can be up to a few million dollars and the venture capitalist (VC) would expect a large ownership in exchange. The funds should be enough to last a couple of years at least and give you a sufficiently long runway—long enough for you to take off for a second-round investment from a second set of VCs. Usually, if you are doing well, the organization is shaping up as something valuable and the relationship with the VC is healthy, your VC will help in getting the next investor.

Each time you raise money, you dilute the ownership of the company. Hence you would have to finely balance the amount of money you raise and the proportionate control you give up. The trick is to raise enough money, well before your current working capital runs out and from the right kind of investors. The process of raising money is full-time work and if you have to do it too often, it is a huge distraction from the actual act of running the organization. So, one must tread this path with care. Choosing the right investor is almost like matrimony. Exciting and perilous. Just as you would not jump into matrimony without due diligence, you do not want to hitch your wagon here without thinking a lot of things through. So, here we go with a few golden rules. I believe, whenever you make any choice, you also choose the consequences. In this chapter, I want to tell you about choosing the right investor, the right way. It is all the more important because there is no science to it and on many counts, you will have to make your call based finally on what your gut feeling says. I know of many ventures gone wrong because the entrepreneur did not do enough due diligence and chose the wrong set of investors.

It is important that you choose investors who understand your business—in other words, stay away from what is called 'dumb capital'. When the word goes around that you are looking for money, a lot of people will offer their money—many will promise that they will not interfere in your work. Non-interference cannot be the reason why you choose to raise money from someone. Anyone who puts in hard-earned money must and will hold you accountable and you better embrace that discipline. It is good for everyone, particularly so for the internal controls, systems and processes that will fall in place when there is fiscal accountability. Once a quarter, a couple of days of concentrated interaction with your investor is essential to the health of the organization.

Some investors will overpromise how much business they will bring in for you and so on. Beware of such promises. Often people confuse the role of the investor with that of a rainmaker—someone who will make your business wildly successful by bringing in loads of business. If you have not figured out by yourself how to sell, do not expect your investor to do that for you. Sometimes, investors do open a door here and a door there. But remember, the act of convincing the customer is for you to do. If your investor brings you an occasional business lead, take that as a bonus. Some investors overplay their ability to get you business. You would do well to largely discount that as a reason for you to choose one over the other.

Some of the real key considerations are the source of capital, the quantum of equity being sought, the quality of participation in board meetings (assuming they have a board position—it depends on what you have negotiated), the accountability being asked for in return for the money and, finally, exit intent and any other special conditions that they might insist upon. Do not leave this process to well-meaning dialogue alone. You would do well to have a good lawyer and an accountant when you negotiate the actual terms closer to the deal making.

Usually, it takes anywhere between six months to a year from the time an investor evinces interest in your proposal to the time the money reaches your bank. There is a lot of involved paper work and negotiations that precede the final transaction. During this period, one must have active alternatives at all times.

Though you should not shop around only on the basis of valuation (how much money in return for how much of ownership you would get) and must be very clear about what kind of investment and investor you are looking for, never take anyone for granted. The deal is not done until the money has hit the bank. It's important not to show desperation. It helps if you have enough money in the bank.

There are investors who may ask that while you are talking to them, you should not talk to anyone else. That is an unreasonable condition and you would do well to tell them that it is not possible to maintain that level of exclusivity unless certain criteria are met from both sides.

Above all else, you must sense the right chemistry with the people dealing with you from the investor's side. If, for some reason, you do not like someone at a personal level early on in the equation and the dislike persists, do not overlook this factor's potential for creating future discord.

I recall, early in our quest for an investor, I had a breakfast meeting scheduled with a leading fund manager who was staying in the same hotel as I. He had asked for the meeting in his room at 8 in the morning. Right on time, I rang the doorbell. When he opened the door, I found him in his pyjamas. To me that was a stupid way to start a relationship. What followed was a fairly patronizing breakfast meeting during which instead of trying to get to know me and the proposed venture, he gave me a pompous view of his own empire. I decided then and there that his company was out of the running. After all, it was a planned business meeting. We were not old buddies. If I could come properly dressed and be on time, he ought to show the same courtesy to me.

The best thing about setting up MindTree was that the chosen investors—Walden International, Global Technology Ventures and subsequently the Capital Group—always treated us as an equal. An entrepreneur is a very special person. He may be a nobody in the beginning, but he deserves to be treated with respect by the potential investor. If respect is missing, the two are not right for each other.

A compatible relationship does not mean unnecessary intimacy. Early in the cycle, Krishna Kumar and I started discussions with an expatriate venture capitalist. He insisted we meet at his home and each time, the prospective investor would prepare a great fare. All this time, he was charming to a fault. In the normal course of things, we had decided, he would have the first right of refusal. But, closer to the point of valuation, the man came up with a number that was very far from what we thought was reasonable. We gave him enough indications of this, but he either ignored them or failed to notice them. As a result, we settled the deal with Walden and Global Technology Ventures on terms both sides found eminently suitable. The VC was so angry that he called me up and threatened that I would hear from his lawyers soon. The man stopped speaking to us in social gatherings and went around predicting doom for us. The moral of the story: be professional yourself and look for professionalism in every dealing, in every small transaction. Do not get carried away by the polite talk and the snacks.

Next, probe the source of funding. Often, it determines how the investors will behave in the future and how they will deal with you as well as support you in times of difficulty. Large venture funds usually raise their money from sources like international financial institutions such as the World Bank, the IMF, large banks, mutual funds, endowments of universities like Harvard, Princeton and Stanford and wealthy individuals. Some in the last category could be successful past or current entrepreneurs themselves who know what is involved.

Dealing with people who have transparent sources of funds is a far better option than turning to questionable sources. A lot of American railroads in the early years were built with gangster money. Even today, there is a lot of such money going around. I would be careful about raising money from people who have questionable sources or are not known for their financial integrity. They may approach you with the promise of non-interference and flexibility with financing options, ease of dealing and a very innocent statement like, 'I do not even understand anything about your business, I want to put in some money because I personally like you and have heard good things about you from others.' Beware. I would rather have an investor who knows my business and is able to appreciate possible downstream complexities than someone who is bound to extend to my business the rules of the game as he practises them. Also, people get to know who is investing in you and the reputation of your present investor often determines the kind of second-round investor you will attract in subsequent years.

I would also be wary of raising money from friends and family who love you but do not understand your business. This is a personal matter though, particularly in countries like India where a lot of new ventures do get built with family money and goodwill. Having said that, I would rather keep affection and business at arm's length, specially if you want to build a professional organization. It helps.

Now, let us shift to what not to trade your equity for. I see this happen quite often. A young technologist wants to start a business. Rightly or wrongly, he thinks that renting a

place is the biggest impediment in setting up a venture—
'Oh, we need an office to begin with'—and he trades equity
with someone who obliges with the space. Or, consider
this—someone promises to help you with legal advice on a
continuing basis, or to get contracts, or whatever. In return
he wants a piece of the pie. Pay in cash for things as much
as you can. Where a loan is available and you can reasonably
afford to repay it, take the loan. Do not use up equity if you
can, explore other avenues. Reason: your equity may have
value beyond your wildest dreams.

Remember, if the company is a sound venture, the
compounded annual appreciation of equity is likely to be
many times higher than the reigning interest rate. So, raising
a loan may be a better idea. Secondly, rather than give out
a share of the company to someone who is promising to get
me a contract, I would rather keep it to hire the best sales
person on the block. Do not fritter away your stocks. Once
given out, they may never come back.

Early-stage investment in the organization brings in
costly cash. In percentage terms, in the beginning, you have
to part with more ownership for less money, simply because
the investor is assuming higher risk. Thus, the cost of that
money is higher than the second or the third round of fund-
raising. That assumes the company has done well and the
market is good. Given that, it is important not to lock up
early-state funds in buying fixed assets like land and building.
Fixed assets attract depreciation and this reduces profitability.
Reduced profitability means reduced valuation in later times.

When we started MindTree, some of us had wanted to
use funds raised through equity to buy land and build a

campus. This is an issue that crops up in every new venture with funds to invest. Ashok Soota joined the founding team when version 1 of the business plan was already in place. He questioned the value of using funds to own land and buildings. He maintained that it is not a good idea to own such assets—it is better to spend that money in R&D, development of talent, opening new sales offices and building the brand in the pre-IPO stage. These would generate higher returns and improve the bottom line.

Finally, if you are able to take the company public, the cost of money falls drastically. Good companies are able to command a premium for the stock they sell and that additional money comes with less dilution. Hence, large-scale capital expenditure using early-state finance may not always be a good idea.

Fiscal prudence is always key to gaining investor respect. This is most pronounced during the pre-valuation days when you are courting the investors. They look for signs of fiscal prudence in the many conversations that you would have as a run-up to the valuation event.

An entrepreneur must not lack knowledge in basic finance before talking to an investor. It may be a good idea to acquire that knowledge through a series of sit-down conversations with an expert, such as a chartered accountant. The ideal thing to do is to choose a founder or bring in an early-state employee with a finance background. So, the message is, do not appear to be fiscally ignorant in front of an investor. All entrepreneurs—even people who start a not-for-profit organization—will do well to understand basic accounting, finance, audit and the principles behind corporate governance. There are many short-term courses available on such topics by leading management schools everywhere, and it is well worth it to attend one. Knowledge of these aspects will not only help you get a good investor, it will also help you to keep the relationship in good shape. And who knows, you may be sitting next to your future venture partner in the same class!

While we are talking about choosing an investor right, it is necessary to understand how venture capitalists—VCs—make money, as there is widespread ignorance about this aspect. VCs make money if and when the company is acquired by another buyer or it goes public. At that time, if the value of the share is higher than the price point at which the VC had subscribed, the VC is able to offload the holding and take the proceeds. After keeping his share for the cost of fund management and profits he must retain, the VC distributes the gains among his own investors. The fundamental difference between a VC and a banker is that the former does not 'loan' money for usury. The VC makes money only if the enterprise makes money and becomes valuable in the eyes of subsequent investors. Out of ten enterprises a VC may fund, it is commonplace to see seven fold up. Two may give a return equal to the interest from a bank deposit and only one goes on to give a significant upside to the VC. Thus, the VC takes enormous risks in choosing the right venture. That is why his investment is known as 'risk capital'.

The reason we need to understand this equation is to appreciate that VCs are not in love with you. They are not in love with your business. They are here, legitimately so, to make money, so that they can go and afford to fund the dream of many more start-ups like your own. As long as they do that job well, we should neither expect affection from them nor think of them as villains. Many failed entrepreneurs think of VCs as villains and use names ranging from snakes to sharks to hyenas for them. Usually, you get the VC you deserve.

In order that a VC is able to justify his existence, he requires what is called an exit option. This is a pre-defined event like a buy-out of the VC's stake by another financial institution or the sale of shares through a public issue. Till that happens, a VC is protective about his investment. At the slightest possibility of mismanagement or failure, VCs get worried. This makes them intervene and, in extreme cases, call for change of management. The best way to handle them is educated engagement—keep them fully, transparently posted at all times. Maintain a professional relationship. Do not ever take a position with them that you know is not truthful.

Just as it is important to look at the source of the VC's fund, it is equally vital to look at which other companies the VC has previously engaged with. In how many has he succeeded in helping the organization all the way to the initial public offer? What value has the VC added in helping, advising and coaching the entrepreneur? Know that you have every right to ask for references, just as the VC will seek references before funding you.

While looking for investors, most entrepreneurs get carried away by the concept of valuation. Who is going to give me the maximum money for the least equity? This is an important consideration, no doubt. However, it is less important than the colour of the money and the professional credibility of the fund. It is very important to pay attention to these so that there are fewer surprises as you go along.

Talking of surprises, there are bound to be many. These can be caused by external events and sometimes due to personal issues between investors and entrepreneurs. But the crucial thing is to maintain a professional relationship and trust, so that differences can be ironed out and unanticipated situations get handled in a collaborative manner.

The last word: try and get an investor who takes the long-term view. It could take as long as five to six years before the organization can provide the exit option. Do not get entangled with people who want a quick and easy way out— it will create a huge drain on top management time and distract it from building the business in the formative period of the organization's life.

MAKING THE PITCH

Many people who have a great idea, go to a venture capitalist and make a passionate pitch. They get a cold response and feel dispirited. They go to another, this time the person shreds the idea to pieces. And, then, the next one. Here are a few golden tips on how to engage with them:

1. Do not seek love at first sight. Do not be disheartened by rejections. Your idea may be great to you, but at first glance, 99 per cent ideas are just that: ideas. Pay attention to the questions the venture capitalist (VC) is asking, take serious note of them, ask if you can meet again after you have found deeper answers.
2. Do not try to impress the VC. Conversations must be mature and responsible. Myths apart, the VC is looking for a potential businessman who will be good for his money. Let the idea, the concept, the thoroughness of the business plan impress. Your own look and feel and accent can follow.
3. Before going to a VC, meet an accountant—showing financial ignorance or lack of preparedness doesn't help.
4. It is always a good idea to do serious, even if small-scale, market research before you meet your VC.
5. The greatest thing a VC wants to hear is that you have an idea and a potential customer. So, it is always a great idea to test-market the concept with a few target customers. The exercise will also tell you about the gaps in the idea.
6. Know your competitive landscape well and think through how you would be different.

7. The VC is looking at the team before looking at the idea. A first-rate team with a second-rate idea is always better than a first-rate idea with a second-rate team. Show the team to the VC.

8. Establish comfort levels before you spill out the complete details of your project.

9. It is not necessary to have an intermediary who takes you to a VC for a fee. If your plans are any good, you really do not need anyone.

10. Be honest—do not say things that you do not really know would work. The VC is looking for integrity and dependability, ahead of competence.

11. Do not make hasty commitments on board composition, rights of exclusivity or even percentage of ownership. Do a comparison if you can.

12. Talk to an entrepreneur, seek advice before inking the deal.

NINE

Getting Good People and Keeping Them

In chapter 4, we talked about choosing the start-up team with care and explained how complementarity of the seed team is a critical element of success. But the seed team alone cannot deliver the mission and vision of the organization. It is here that attracting and retaining professional talent becomes the next important thing. You may have a great product or a service idea, you may be able to raise the seed money and buy technology and build infrastructure. None of this is of any value unless there is continuous top-management engagement to attract and retain talent. In today's hyper-competitive world, the war for talent precedes the war for market share. Given that, where should one start?

When we started MindTree in 1999, we paid extraordinary attention to the first forty critical positions in the company. We felt that if we chose the first forty MindTree Minds right, treated them well and empowered them, they would in turn take care of the first four hundred. That is how the concept of fractal leadership works in building an organization. If one does not pay attention to this, scale becomes difficult to achieve. Building sustainable businesses is all about building scale.

While looking for talent in certain functions, one has to be extra careful. In the beginning, we spent an enormous amount of time on this, looking at many candidates before settling on key positions in Quality, Finance, Marketing, Sales, the People Function and Training—we call it Culture and Competency (C2). But filling up senior positions with the right kind of people requires one basic discipline. You must have a written job description for each role and a clear articulation of what kind of competency is needed to fulfil the role. This not only helps to be objective about the choice of the individual but also gives the incumbent a sense of professionalism. When looking for a functional head, you may come across someone who is good but has growing up to do. Do not commit the job title—you can always tell the person that if he or she matures well enough, the title will follow. If you think the person has a lot of growing up to do, be honest about it. Say that he could start off with the job but sooner or later, you expect a more senior person to take overall charge and under that person, you do see growth for the incumbent.

When we were starting MindTree, to most of the incumbents of the first forty critical positions, one of the founders personally presented the mission, vision, values and business plan of the company at the selection stage. We spent individual time with them. We sought a value match, a sense of destiny, strong competence, ability to multitask and resilience. To each, we spoke about the inherent risks of working in a start-up company. We made sure that we were straightforward in dealing with their questions and issues.

Not everyone is cut out to work in a start-up organization. Early in the life of MindTree, I wrote down what I thought were the nine elements needed to work successfully in a start-up organization (see box at the end of the chapter). It is imperative that such issues are discussed with prospective candidates so that they come with their eyes open. You will be surprised how much people value that. It helps attract a very special kind of talent and builds trust from the beginning.

Once people are in, it is important to give them their objectives, provide them the freedom to co-create the organization and hold them accountable. Many start-up organizations implode because people tread too much on each other's toes and a laissez-faire style sets in. The best thing we did at MindTree was to pretend from the first day that we were indeed a big company. So, everyone—chairman included—had to settle annual objectives and submit quarterly reports. Peers were actively encouraged to copy each other in on their reports. Later on, Ashok started a practice of adding a qualitative note after the quarterly report on what went well and what did not. Nothing binds people better than trust, freedom, accountability and stretch.

Two things were clear to us from the beginning. Just by virtue of being a founder one would not be entitled to any special privileges or accelerated career growth. All founders agreed that they were willing to report to a non-founder if the job so required. The second thing we all agreed was that none of our immediate blood relations would ever work for MindTree. These two things go a long way in setting the tone of professionalism in any organization. In all the six years we have been together, not a single spouse has had anything to do with MindTree, and none of our children have ever interned or done a summer job at MindTree either. If any of them ever visit us at the workplace, they have to report at the security desk, sign a register, get a badge and come in and leave accompanied by an escort.

The best way to make an organization opaque is to bring in relatives. However qualified and competent they may be, the presence of kith and kin can create challenges in a professional environment. If you have a brother-in-law on your board or your son is an intern, they will come with the relationship written on their forehead in fluorescent ink. Even if they choose to eat in the company cafeteria, people still get the message: they are special status.

One thing that creates particular heartburn in the early stages is disparities in compensation. Right from the beginning, create a competency-based matrix and let the wage administration be done by a professional. In MindTree, most compensation issues are settled by the People Function. The role of top management is to create the compensation philosophy, issue periodic guidelines, provide oversight on industry benchmarks and resolve the occasional disparity. We do not handle compensation issues as largesse. Once people know that the system does not play favourites, most problems are prevented from happening.

The next thing to do is lead the way with personal

examples of stretch, productivity and accountability. I am an amateur photographer. I get my rolls developed at one of Bangalore's professional studios. It is a place swarming with people—customers and technicians and counter clerks. It is owned by one man. One day, I arrived early as the place was opening for the day. I sat there, watching the flow of events. First came the cleaning staff. Then came the minions. Then came the counter clerks and much later, the technicians. The owner was the last man to enter the studio. He went round the place looking at various activities before settling into his high chair in the only cubicle in the store. He is the proprietor. He owns the place. By the very nature of his ownership, he works a little less than his employees have to. This man makes a lot of money. He has a successful business as long as he will live, but he cannot ever build an institution. In some proprietor-driven businesses, it may be okay to work less than the employees, or keep a different yardstick of personal behaviour and accountability. Not so if you are to create a professionally managed, high-performance organization. In it, *you* are not the employer. The business is.

I can never overstate the importance of five things in managing high-performance professionals: set up a performance management system that everyone understands, communicate with people with evangelical regularity, listen to the voice of your people through formal and regular perception surveys that are conducted by an outside agency, focus on development of leadership and, finally, create a support network for your leaders. If an organization knows how to do these five things right, it can scale without breaking up and will have less of a challenge in attracting and retaining good talent as it moves forward.

Competent people often join a start-up because it is the next best thing to starting out on their own. Some of them, however, achieved their past success working in a large organization and may find performing in a start-up not all that simple. Sometimes, people can be starry-eyed and romanticize the idea of making it happen in a start-up. Sooner rather than later, they could become a liability. If you sense this in someone, get him to brace the hard work through clear objectives and get on with serving real customers. Budget for some transplant failures of this kind.

There are also those outstanding people who, for some reason, need an emotional safety net of sorts and do not feel confident of doing their own thing. Rather, they prefer to live their start-up dream by working in one. They need to be understood, nurtured and valued. Without them, there is no way one can build a great organization. Some of the important aspects of working with such people are: stretch goals, freedom, constant communication, encouragement in risk-taking and creation of a strong peer group. The last one is very important, particularly given the roller-coaster ride a start-up inevitably goes through. Let us talk about each of these with particular care. In a way, you may say, this is all textbook stuff that any organization needs to follow in any case. In 'any organization' they may be good principles to follow. In a fledgling organization, they can mean the difference between success and total failure. Let me pick a few of the important aspects.

First, let us talk about the need for constant

communication. You can never overcommunicate. There is no such thing. Yet, people get so busy with themselves, they do not even realize when they have stopped communicating. Communicating is not informing, yet informing is a starting point.

If the founding team has figured out everything and all it needs is a bunch of order-takers, why should brilliant people take the risk of working in a start-up? People seek inclusion in strategy and problem solving. Towards this, you have to constantly inform them of issues, problems, opportunities and concerns. For this, they must have access to information at all times—even when it is inconvenient.

At MindTree, we use the 95:95:95 principle. Ashok Soota came up with the principle behind the idea. According to him, 95 per cent of the people must get access to 95 per cent of the information, 95 per cent of the time. Providing such a flood of information is possible only with an electronic infrastructure like a good intranet system that is content-rich. The 95:95:95 principle does create one problem in a venture-funded start-up. Venture capitalists do not like financial information to be available to all and sundry. Also, start-ups are not comfortable talking about their issues and concerns. Some prefer to keep them under wraps and look at any source of light with feelings of insecurity.

There could be perfect reasons for seeking such privacy, but with competent people around, you cannot shroud yourself in secrecy. They just hate it. So, the best way is to negotiate upfront with investors at the level of information-sharing they are comfortable with. Know, however, that some of them do not really understand the human side of building an organization. Thus, you have to get it out of them and also, progressively increase their comfort level so that you can build an increasingly transparent organization.

The next issue is about nurturing risk-taking in the team. In start-ups, the risk-taking ability of the entrepreneur is often over-rated. It is not his or her ability alone but the collective risk-taking ability that defines the character of the organization. How do you encourage people to take risks?

Consider three things. Give them a job when they are only 60 per cent ready for it. Two, allow them to fumble and make mistakes—sometimes, very expensive mistakes. Three, rotate the top performers at least once in two to three years. The charm of a start-up is that it can create many start-ups within a start-up. Imagine a young MBA joining an established company's marketing team. That can never give her the same thrill that she would get in creating a marketing department in a young organization from scratch. That thrill, no money can buy. There is a certain beauty, a very special charm, when a plant is just a sapling with all of three leaves. No mighty oak can match that. Entrepreneurs must understand the currency of that spirit. Remember, for a long time, being a start-up within a start-up will remain a sought-after experience. Your people will want to say, 'I started the London office, I created the first intranet portal, I hired the first employee for the travel vertical, I closed the first accounting year!'

As start-ups grow and deal with many different challenges, it becomes very important to create an internal support group, a network of sorts for the high-performance professionals. In MindTree, we have a Leadership Team that receives regular, formal communication on issues from the top team. It meets Ashok at least once in forty-five days. The team is listened to and respected. This team's development needs are specially focused on and they are encouraged to build their own network. This becomes a critical support system because it is not possible to refer to the top each time. Sometimes, they need their own 'sense-making' structure.

In most start-ups, inadequate attention is paid to the subject of leadership development. Early on, we created a homespun training program called the MindTree Leader's Program. This in-house development program was extended to all the senior people and as the organization kept growing, it was repeated to several sets of new leaders. In 2004, we scrapped it because we felt that no leadership development program could be future-proof. We assembled the top team and asked them what were the desired traits in the newer breed of leaders they expected to see. Once that input was synthesized, we chalked out a new structure. This time around, we asked the same set of leaders to design a series of case studies based on actual MindTree experience. For this, we went to Prof. N. Balasubramanian at the Indian Institute of Management, Bangalore, who came and taught them the art of writing and teaching case studies. Thereafter, the same set of leaders designed a unique program, got peer review done and then rolled it out to more than 700 young leaders. The uniquely designed program was christened 'Leading Performance' and consisted of very innovative modules like contextual visioning of teams, managing over- and underachievers, dealing with adversity and so on.

A workplace is a social microcosm. In it, people learn best when the learning is voluntary. Consequently, we created a Knowledge Management (KM) organization under Raj Datta, whose life's mission was to work in the area of KM. The KM organization built more than thirty communities of practice, an entirely volunteer-driven effort which focused on human capital management. They chose their own areas of interest, created their own agenda, chose their own leaders, decided on when and where they would meet. The responsibility of the management is to provide physical and electronic infrastructure, coffee and snacks, some reward and recognition and generally stay out of the way. This set off a wave of organizational initiatives and created a collegial atmosphere. An enormous amount of innovation sprang out of their activities. So much energy was generated through the communities that in 2005, we decided to present the organization for an intellectual capital rating to IC Sweden. IC Sweden, born out of pioneering work done at Skandia, in Stockholm, assesses the intellectual capital of an organization, in the same way people assess the financial capital and publish it as a balance sheet. When the assessment came out, we were rated among the top 12 per cent in the world, across industries, in terms of the value of our intellectual capital that consists of human capital, structural capital and customer capital.

One of the challenges in creating a high-growth organization is always assimilation. In most young organizations, it happens in an ad hoc manner. It is seldom geared to meet varying needs and in most places, there is a one-size-fits-all approach. Assimilation is the starting point of an engagement and if done well, not only adds to the retention rate, but it actually unleashes new energy which¯ every new employee wants to bring in. In MindTree, C2 takes care of the assimilation of people who join us from the campus. It is roughly about 30 per cent of our newly joined workforce. That creates an interesting challenge, because a vast majority of people are 'lateral hires'—meaning people with previous work experience. This is a fragile group because they bring in their past ways of doing things, feel a sense of loss right after joining and are most given to attrition.

To handle this group, we pulled out Sanjay Selvankar and Shrish Kulkarni, two outstanding managers, and gave them a free hand. When you take in a new employee from the campus and train him or her in your way of doing things, it is akin to growing a sapling from a seed. It is easier to do this as compared to assimilating a lateral employee who is more like an uprooted, grown-up plant and hence, likely to wilt before finding new roots. The result was the creation of a program called 'Arboretum', which means a botanical garden devoted to trees. Sanjay and Shrish conceptualized a role-based, tiered assimilation structure for the laterals—we even created a protective environment for them with its own special infrastructure. There, a new hire came in, settled into the organization's way of doing things and once comfortable, was assigned project responsibilities. The result was a dramatic shift in assimilation success as well as subsequent retention.

Lastly, I want to talk to you about the importance of shared vision, values and wealth creation. People do not want to subscribe to handed-down vision and value statements. At least the first few hundred people must be fully engaged in the design of the vision and the values. They have to be able to say, 'I wasn't just there, I was part of the process through which the vision and values were formalized.' That is the best way of making it a memorable journey for a high-performance team. When something is memorable, it is most likely to spread itself and then, fractalize all over again. In the process, you discover that one day it is no longer the three-leaf sapling. It has actually become the giant oak.

When that time arrives, people must feel that they were suitably rewarded for making it happen. The way to do it is to upfront settle the amount of ownership that must go in as an Employee Stock Option Plan (ESOP). This book is not a primer on how to set one up, how to administer it equitably and what the accounting issues involved are. The amount of ownership that must be kept aside for people depends on the compensation and benefit philosophy, the nature of the business and how long you want the pool to last. It is important you pay attention to these and set up clear-cut guidelines on how the pool is to be treated, what are the lock-in and buy-back processes.

It is important that founders do not administer the ESOP themselves—it must be done by professionals within the system. It is also critical that the founders do not dip into the employee stock option plan themselves.

Having said all that, I must also caution you that stock grants have their limitations too. Do not expect stock options to be *the* solution for all ownership issues. Peter Drucker made a profound statement once. He said that things like stock option plans work only in good times. In tough times, they do not. People need a much bigger reason than money alone to give their best to an organization. As you build the company, every time there is a serious issue like attrition, inability to attract talent or internal dissatisfaction over some issue that proves hard to settle, people will come and tell you to issue more stock options. It is a stupid thing to do. It is not a substitute for fixing systemic problems and does not earn any goodwill if stocks are simply doled out. Employee stock options must be generous. But each time they are distributed, they should have been earned well.

WORKING FOR A START-UP
Nine things you should know

(In the early days at MindTree, this was compulsory reading for new entrants)

1. It means dealing with risk and sharing rewards

Working for a start-up is not for the weak at heart. The reason is simple. For every start-up that succeeds, more struggle and some more fail. Only a small percentage of the voyagers who leave the shore succeed. Secondly, when we look at the big successes, we generally get carried away by the outward manifestations of success and do not consider the blood, sweat and tears that went into achieving the success and are not in the public gaze. Consider this—when Infosys was started, the founders did not find a bank that would give them a working capital arrangement. Worse, when the company went public, its issue was undersubscribed. The bottom line in every start-up is 'risk'. If you do not enjoy it, a start-up is not for you. The upside of making your way from an early stage to a successful start-up is, of course, quite significant. Both in terms of professional learning and wealth creation opportunity, a start-up is an excellent place. However, there is a caveat—the harvest is a story of postponed gratification.

2. The harvest comes only in the long haul

Normally, a start-up takes anywhere from three to five years to come to a stage where it can go public and only after that, employees can reap the harvest of their hard work. It is quite commonplace for both sweat equity and employee stock options to have vesting that spreads over three to five years. As a result, it becomes necessary to develop a state of mind that accepts a career marathon. This is a very important consideration because in India, the average software developer has two years of experience and has a track record of 1.75 job changes. Given that propensity, if a software developer works for very short periods, the completeness of a start-up experience will not occur, nor would the person benefit financially. After all, the reason to join a start-up is to gain larger learning and to make money through stock options. Thus if an individual is more comfortable surfing jobs, it is probably better to keep hopping between large, established organizations.

3. You should be the type who can work unsupervised— remember, you are the system

This is a very important issue—before jumping into a start-up ask yourself whether you work best under supervision or are able to create your own work, structure it and deliver it with minimal supervision or none at all. If yes, come right in. If you are unsure, continue in the big, faceless company that can afford supervision.

In a start-up, at times it happens that even if supervision could add value, people are so busy multitasking that no one can really ensure that you are doing your work or let you know every now and then that you are directionally correct. The ability to work unsupervised, the ability to reach out and ask for help are critical requirements. If a person walks into the office in the morning and says, 'Show me my boss and tell me what to do today', he or she will find a start-up a very difficult place to work in.

4. Construct the big picture, focus on the small

People who can make it big in a start-up are those who can see the big picture and at the same time, sharply focus on the small—the one on which today depends critically. The big picture is important because that is where the company is going. It may take a few years but that is what binds everyone together. Usually, it is just a map, a business plan or a statement of vision. It is not the exact, guaranteed future itself. Imagine that you are a discoverer. You set sail in search of unknown lands. What you will have for most of the journey is only a map. Not the reality. Given that fact, it takes a lot of strength to get emotional sustenance from a piece of paper or an overall purpose that the team is trying to achieve.

While the ability to perceive the big picture is important, equally important is the need for staying focused on the immediate deliverables. After all, the future is many todays, strung together in time.

Given that, it is very important to have faith in what I am doing today and the knowledge that done well, it will indeed take me to my destiny. The ability to focus on today while moving towards tomorrow is an uncommon quality that is a pre-requisite for being happy working in a start-up.

5. Teamwork is critical

A lot of people in the software business prefer to work in isolation. A survey conducted some time ago indicated that the average Indian software professional is relatively low on teamwork. Yet, more than any other place, a start-up requires a tremendous amount of teamwork. By definition, a start-up has fewer hands and more things to be done. Everyone has to share the load of a lot of undefined work that cannot wait. As a result, there has to be a willingness to share the load in a new organization.

At MindTree, for example, everyone cleans up after lunch, everyone picks up the phone or fixes the server when it goes down or runs down to get a photocopy done. Similarly, the need to take care of customer requirements or teaching each other is so high that no one waits to be told that it needs to be done. Those who do not appreciate the importance of teamwork or do not enjoy it will find it hard to adjust.

6. Things do not work as per the plan—do not get flustered

If you ask me to make one cardinal observation, it is going to be this one. When you start a company, you begin with many assumptions. You assume that person 'A' is your friend, you assume that a long-standing customer will do business with you, you assume that the banker you know so well will put your project proposal in the fast lane and, of course, you assume that you will raise your first fat invoice and get paid in record time.

None of that will actually happen. Rest assured.

The excitement of an enterprise is precisely that. Because none of that happens, the people in a start-up try out different customer propositions, recruitment strategies, funding plans and alliances. In the process, they innovate, and those who do it right make it big. However, the process quite often is a roller-coaster ride. As things fail to happen per plan, there is the inevitable period of confusion, self-doubt and unpaid bills. A start-up is for those who will create new maps and be willing to explore new paths, and not for those who prefer a guided tour of the future.

7. You must have faith in yourself—you need to contribute to the energy, not depend on it

What personality trait is required to cope with high highs and low lows? A lot of self-confidence. A start-up needs people who believe in themselves. People who know that irrespective of the outcome, at a personal level they will emerge rich in experience—if the start-up gets grounded, they would still be able to resurrect their lives and move on. There are many of us who seek confidence from the environment we live in; we depend largely on a feedback process to sustain ourselves. On the other hand, there are many who recognize the presence of the environment, accept its generosity, but at a basic level, thrive on their inner sense of worth. In a sense, these are nuclear-powered people. More than any place else, a start-up depends on the energy that such people bring to the organization and unless that paradigm is recognized, it can be a very discomforting proposition.

8. Learn to accept a low-resource work environment

At MindTree Consulting right now, there are more people than chairs, desktops and notebooks. For those who go to war only if heavily accessorized, a start-up is not the place. The very fact that we are a start-up implies that our resource base is much smaller than big and established players. More than them, we have to watch costs, worry about prioritizing expenses and postpone gratification in a real personal sense. After all, we need to respect the confidence of the investors. People need to mentally accept that infrastructural support will go down several notches, and for those who would rather not give up their corporate lifestyle or feel lost without a glitzy life support system, a start-up is avoidable.

9. Big joy in small things

Now if all that we talked about is true, then where is the fun? Where is the joy in a start-up? It is in the small things. It is only in a start-up that there is no corporate caste system. There is no way you can look at someone and say what his or her level is. Everyone pitches in, everyone fights, everyone pulls weight and people are still not busy enough to be in silos that prevent rapid cross-fertilization of knowledge, skills and attitudes. It is also in a start-up that you can correlate your contribution to organizational impact. People instantly know who did it.

A start-up is also a place where no one has time for politics. You survive one day at a time. There is the joy of accelerated learning, the opportunity to watch people at close quarters and get a participant's view of how businesses are built. If all goes well, along the line comes the satisfaction of creating substantial personal wealth that is difficult for most people through the salaried route. Finally, all these come in addition to a unique sense of bonding that money cannot buy.

TEN

Building the Process-focused Organization

The birth of an organization is a creative process. Only creative people start companies. While there is no denying the fact that starting something new is a creative act and requires a very generative, nurturing mindset, there is a general misconception that the essence of the start-up process is devoid of process-oriented thinking and action.

This misconception is amplified by the popular, romanticized ideas about incubation. After all, Hewlett-Packard was started in a garage and Microsoft was the result of two kids tinkering with their Atari computer. While it may be that chaotic circumstances lead to ideation and sometimes a company is born out of that churn, what must follow is a well-thought-out and often rapid movement towards establishing a process-focused organization.

Most start-ups hit a glass ceiling sooner or later because they fail to respect the power of process. If you look at any organization that has become something of substantial value for others, you will invariably see how it used the power of process to build itself. Sometimes, people use the term 'process-overhead' to reinforce the process-avoidance mindset. It becomes synonymous with something like a regimen. Think of process as going to a gym regularly and doing yoga and watching your diet so that you grow up healthy. You have to do all of it as a conscious investment in yourself rather than a regimen.

Long back, I was listening to a lecture by a Japanese process expert from Fuji Xerox. It used to be a joint venture between Fuji and Xerox. Fuji Xerox won the legendary Deming Prize for Total Quality Management even before Xerox, the parent company, got the Malcolm Baldridge Award for quality in the US. The gentleman was explaining why process orientation is key to building competitive success. Someone asked him vainly, 'But Michelangelo followed no process?'

Unflustered, the expert replied, 'First be Michelangelo.' Everybody else, he said, must follow process.

Then he went on to explain that though Michelangelo may not have needed process, but to make the 100,000th flawless reprint of his work, we could not do without process.

I would argue that all creative people at that level actually have a strong process orientation, only their version of process is not apparent to the untrained eye. So, if you are looking at building anything memorable, you have to understand and respect process.

Building a company is about growth. Growth of new ideas, products, services, people, distribution channels, internal systems and procedures. While growth is fundamental to survival, all growth is inherently destructive—it usually involves a tussle between centripetal and centrifugal forces. One set of imperatives wants to get away from the core and expand at the seams. Another set of forces wants to hold on to the core. The way to grow without breaking apart in this churn is to build process. It is akin to creating a high-rise structure, but before doing that we need to make sure that there are strong beams and columns. Without these, the system collapses under its own weight. Process works like the beams and the columns.

In many ways, process is also like plumbing. It cannot be an afterthought. As in so many of our cities, where the buildings come up first and then planners wake up to the need for an effective drainage system and availability of parking space. These cannot be afterthoughts, just as you cannot imagine first putting together a building and then thinking about the capacity and layout of the plumbing system. You have to frontload process into the organization-building activity.

Before going further, I have to tell you something basic. Process is not about compliance. It is not about what is called 'certification hunting'. A lot of people think of it as quality certification—getting an ISO 9001 or a SEI CMMi or a PCMM initiative rolling in the company with the sole intent of hanging the plaque on the wall or meeting the qualifying criteria of a bid. While such assessments or certifications are helpful in getting business, they must be embraced in the right spirit—each of these is to be taken as a means to an end. The end is about creating an organization that will outlive its initial charter, its founding team and remain both memorable and valuable for everyone connected to it or touched by it.

This means, building a process-focused organization must be part of the top management's vision. They must see it in every small aspect of the organization's functioning and lead by example. This requires the top management to learn the fundamentals of quality, choose the right process leadership to work out and implement a process framework in the organization and personally review process deployment and adherence at each step. As long as the enterprise lives, one cannot take one's eyes off it.

At MindTree, we started with a very well-thought-out process deployment plan from the very beginning in all the people-related areas because our business is people-centric and people intensive. So, all aspects of recruitment, compensation and benefits, objective setting and performance evaluation were worked out and made applicable to everyone from the start itself.

In order to ensure that the right financial processes fell in place, great attention was paid to the format and periodicity of financial reports. For delivery, we went about carefully looking at all available talent and finally zeroed in on our choice—Vishweshwar Hegde, who had been closely associated with Motorola's SEI CMM deployment and Six Sigma initiatives. He was made to report directly to the chairman of the company so that the legitimacy of the function was never in doubt. In turn, Vishweshwar hand-picked a group of highly committed process experts. He also enlisted the entire leadership team and involved them in designing a delivery process that is 'practitioner-defined and practitioner-led'. He conceptualized a quality triad that consists of three things, people, process and technology, that remains at the core of what we have focused on during all these years.

The key thing about building process centricity in an organization is to pretend that you are a big company right from the start. If you pretend to be a grown-up, you use bigger benchmarks and inevitably gravitate towards self-improvement. MindTree is a good example of such pretence.

In building process centricity, the most important thing is to begin with the voice of the customer. For us, there are two sets of customers: the internal customers who are our own people and the external customers who pay for our products and services and are the reason for our existence. With both sets of customers, we check periodically what they think of us.

The external customer survey is conducted by the in-house quality team once every six months—here we feel that a year is too long a time for something so important. We look at various parameters of customer experience and use a five-point scale to gauge satisfaction, taking into account only four and above as signs of positive experience so that we do not get lulled into complacence. All strategy meetings in the company, which are chaired by Ashok, begin with Vishweshwar's presentation on the state of quality as seen by the customer.

Similarly, early in the game, we tied up with Professor Sumita Raghuram, who is now at Penn State University and was earlier at Fordham University in New York. She is a management teacher who focuses on organizational behaviour and design. She has been conducting the MindTree People Perception Study (MPPS) year after year. The idea was that her 'outside-in' view would be useful to us, while on her side she could gain interesting insights into how organizations evolve. Most great companies are studied only after they achieve greatness. Her idea was to see a work in progress that could become great one day.

The important thing about listening to the voice of the customer is that it must then be transmitted to all parts of the organization, without shame and embarrassment when failures take place or too much self-glorification when there are outstanding successes.

There are bound to be uncomfortable truths about the organization that will emerge. So, what happens if your investors, your prospective customers and worse, your competition get to know what is wrong with you? Irrespective of this, one must share the feedback openly and help the organization come out with corrective measures. Hiding information from your own people is a lot worse than admitting that there are areas where the organization needs to improve. For one, the negative impact of such information reaching your people through other sources will be much greater. Secondly, it betrays a certain lack of self-confidence.

While formal, structured surveys conducted with religious regularity are a must, it is equally important that these are followed up with visible and vigorous improvement, else respondents quickly lose interest in participating in the feedback process. Whenever a survey throws up a negative feedback, a personal phone call, a face-to-face meeting to acknowledge the feedback and explain the follow-up action works like a miracle.

Having said all that, no satisfaction survey can substitute the power of 'face time' with customers. It is the time senior people across the organization spend meeting prospects and customers. There is also no substitute to top management engagement—all members of MindTree's internal board spend at least 40 to 60 per cent of their time either with customers in the field or with MindTree Minds. Many of these meetings are unstructured and without a formal agenda. No feedback is seen as trivial or discounted. One needs to prioritize action but nothing should be dismissed just because it comes from a particular source or is uncomfortable in its import. Such feedback is distributed among all of us internally.

The reason you want to constantly listen to the voice of the customer is that it is an opportunity to improve—sometimes in a breakthrough manner. However, that alone does not suffice. There is a continuous need to do two other things: to look out and study best practices from other organizations, and to learn from unusual sources. While comparing with others, there may be a tendency to aim low, using the size and age of the start-up as a justification. Again, I must say, pretend you are very big. Being big is not about size, it is about mindset.

In embracing the organizational process journey, the critical choice people must make is, whose process? I believe that leaders must be fully involved in the process definition. While it is necessary that processes and tools that fit the organization need not be reinvented and may exist elsewhere, there is greater chance of acceptance and subsequent opportunity to improve if these processes are practitioner-defined and practitioner-led, that is, people who would have to live with the process must be the ones involved with the process definition itself. Today's electronic infrastructure like portals and intranets make process framework design and deployment easier far easier than they ever were before. The greater the electronicization of the organization, easier is the process deployment. Sometimes, early-state companies feel shy of making a seemingly large investment in creating an electronic infrastructure right in the beginning. But it pays for itself many times over as the company grows.

That brings us to another interesting point. How long do we have to worry about process? There is a marvellously apt Japanese story I heard during my early days in quality. It was told to me by a Japanese quality expert. The story goes like this: A monk was tending to a Japanese garden and meticulously, for hours on end, he was removing dry twigs from the immaculately maintained flowering bushes. A passer-by, who was fascinated by the complete concentration and care of the monk at work, could no longer hold himself. He asked the monk, 'O holy one, when will your work be done?' Without looking up, the monk replied, 'When the last dry twig is removed from the garden.' An organization, like a garden, is a living thing, and the process of removing dry twigs never ends. So, like the monk, the top management can never say, the job is done.

In the process journey, embracing a framework like ISO 9001 or SEI CMMi or whatever makes most sense is very important. But these certifications are like good seed. Planting seed, however good it might be, on infertile soil will not work. The fertility of the soil must be checked before the seeds are sown. In an organizational context, that fertility condition is about the right culture. The job of the founding team is to set that right culture and then tend to it like the Japanese monk.

At MindTree, as a software services company, we embraced SEI CMM as a delivery-process framework and took the organization to level 3 during the first three years of the organization. Thereafter, we prioritized the adoption of what is called the People Capability Maturity Model (PCMM) that focuses on people processes and after achieving level 5 in it (we became the youngest company in the world at that time to be assessed at level 5), we went back to further work on SEI CMMi—a latter framework beyond the original SEI CMM model focused on overall delivery quality—and reached the level 5 goal in it.

Every organization must think through its own quality journey and there are enough knowledge and resources available today on the subject. What is missing is the secret sauce that only the founding team and the top management can provide through personal involvement and rigour.

Let me conclude this chapter by pointing out a fatal flaw in process adoption. I always tell people that in upcoming organizations, the P/E ratio is very important. Any MBA or accountant will tell you that conventionally, this stands for price/earning ratio of the share. No, I am not talking about that. To me, P/E stands for Process to Empathy. Neither process is a substitute for empathy, nor empathy alone can enable scaling—reaching increasingly larger volumes of growth—as the organization expands. We need to be dually committed—dually driven to raise a beautiful organization. Like the Japanese garden.

ELEVEN

A Company Is Known by the Customers It Keeps

As a child, remember your parents telling you, 'A man is known by the company he keeps?' Remember how they used to tell you to choose your friends wisely? The warm smile on their faces each time you brought home a studious and talented friend? How Mother would eagerly open the refrigerator for that kid?

On the other hand, when you wanted permission to go out with someone who was not exactly seen as a 'beneficial influence' on you, how concerned they used to be?

The reason your parents always advised you to choose your friends right was that their excellence as well as their mediocrity had high chances of rubbing off on you.

No one told you this before: it is the same with your customers.

Your customers' excellence and their mediocrity rubs off the same way on your organization. Good companies and good customers tend to gravitate towards each other. Likewise, getting paired with a wrong customer can set you back and you could lose huge opportunity being caught in a 'deadly embrace'. So, choose your customers well. Not everyone is meant to be paired with everyone else. The relationship with customers has a very wide and deep impact on the evolving personality of a nascent organization, just like the ninth-grade friendship with the kid next door changed the way you looked at maths, sports or human relationships!

Many years back, when I was chief executive of Wipro's Global R&D, Sath Sathyanarayana, at that time the International Program Manager at Tandem's R&D, asked me, 'How do you choose your customers?' I really did not know how to answer his question.

More to save face, I told him four factors that would govern my choice. As the years have gone by, I have deeply begun to believe in those four factors. I realize how meaningful the inadvertent discovery was. The four factors are: the 'techno-managerial' value that a customer brings to the table; trust; a sense of equality in day-to-day dealings; and finally, a commercially win-win deal, in that order.

The first factor is about opportunity gain or loss beyond the contracted value of a given deal. This particularly involves companies in the services arena. Beyond getting paid for the work we do, who we work for makes a huge difference in terms of learning for the organization. That learning could have a disproportionate impact on the organization. The result is inner growth, with which a company remains ahead of the curve and is able to continuously improve its products and services. Every customer has huge potential to add to the techno-managerial competence of the serving company.

A little critique here, a minor feedback there, a gentle rap on the knuckles can lead to significant development of the people who are engaged in the relationship from your side.

As a result, they emerge from the customer engagement a lot taller, more knowledgeable and more self-confident. These end up being your stock-in-trade. These days, there is a lot of talk about Knowledge Management (KM). KM evangelists will tell you that the job of an enterprise is to build value. Towards this, it has three kinds of capital: human capital, intellectual capital and customer capital. The three enrich each other and have high co-dependency.

On the other hand, if you work with a well-paying customer who doesn't add much techno-managerial value, you emerge intellectually poorer. That engagement has poor leverage and little long-term value. The time spent could mean an opportunity loss. There is no way one can regain the lost time in the process. Thus, when making a deal or weighing a concession during a negotiation, I always look for how much a proposed relationship would help my people grow.

The second factor is trust. In business, everyone talks about it, but few perceive it as something tangible. But, we need to think again. I have come to believe that trust drives cycle-time. Given trust, your cycle-time in any transaction comes down drastically.

The more 24/7 your operation, the more globally dispersed your supply chain, higher becomes the need to look at trust as a cycle-time issue. Take a simple example.

A customer calls you up and says his house is on fire. Would you rush your best man there? If the relationship lacks trust, you might think the customer is telling you there is a fire when, possibly, all there is is just smoke. By the same token, when he asks for help, if you did not trust him well enough, you would conclude that the matter could well wait for the next day.

On the other hand, where trust exists, I have seen miracles happen.

Imagine, you have entered into a contract in good faith but at the time of making the deal, both sides had inadequate information. In executing that contract, somewhere downstream, you are hurting. You tell your customer that it is hurting you. If there is no trust, the customer will show you the contract and plead helplessness in solving your problem. If there is trust, the same person will move mountains to restore fairness in the agreement. We live in an increasingly complex world. More and more organizations today recognize that the contract you write cannot provide guidance on every possible outcome. This makes determining the trust-building ability a critical qualifying factor in choosing your customer.

For young organizations, in most dealings, it is the customer who has the upper hand. In institutional business, chances are high that the customer is also the larger corporate entity. People who deal with you from that end, often make it obvious that the two sides are unequal players in the game. Sometimes, such customers demand deference ahead of quality products or competent service delivery. Some entrepreneurs play along and end up reinforcing such customer behaviour. In deferential relations, the customer progressively loses the capability to take 'no' as an answer.

This can sometimes create devastating consequences. The so-called supplier or vendor, given to serving the customer with servility ahead of efficiency, quickly learns to hide the bad news. He does not question the customer's occasional poor judgement that can have harmful consequences.

It takes a great amount of egoless behaviour on the part of a larger party to set the ground rules ahead of time, to explain to all concerned that the contracted business outcome is more important than pleasing someone in the system. It is true that a supplier has to 'earn' the equal treatment through demonstrated competence. Having said that, when a relationship is started on the basis of equality, the sense of openness, collaboration and ownership can lead to a huge win-win situation. Fear and sycophancy are seldom capable of producing an endurable outcome. Many buying organizations understand these things. Some do not. The rubber usually meets the road when things run into unanticipated difficulty. Who loses? The supplier does. So does the buyer. It is therefore critical that we determine the extent of fair play and equality in the customer's way of doing things.

Finally, let us talk about the last factor—a commercially win-win deal. What is a commercially win-win deal? Simply put, it is a deal that will survive the players sitting around the negotiating table, long after they are all gone. If both sides pay attention to the survivability of a transaction, everything else will just fall into place. Both buyers and sellers can be notoriously capable of taking a short-term or a tactical view of an engagement.

For a start-up, eagerness to 'buy' business is often the cause behind transactions that do not survive the players. Sometimes you do 'buy' business. You do so by agreeing to waive knowledge transfer fees while taking up a project that requires investment of time from your side. You do that because that is the only way to displace the competition that has been in there for ages. You also buy business when you agree to some other similar special concession that is intrinsically not good for you, like giving away equity in exchange of assured business or deeply discounting your price and agreeing to work below cost, as an entry strategy. If you have to buy business, you must do so with eyes open and all consequences well thought-out. Do not buy business at any and all costs. If you do, the chances are low that the deal would be a good one for you.

Win-win deals are reference worthy. It is commonly understood that the seller is the one who is in search of a good reference. After all, his business depends on what we all know as word of mouth. No deal, however large or small, happens today without a reference check with an existing customer or a past one. What people do not realize is how it works the other way round too.

Suppliers build up a collective social memory about customers as well. As a result, they use varying standards of dealings depending on the reputation of the buying organization. Sometimes, good suppliers actually stay away from certain kinds of customers.

Sometimes the buyer-seller role gets swapped. Consider, a senior R&D professional or a marketing chief decides to change jobs. For top-level job changes, prospective employers often do reference checks with suppliers. What about the person's alliance-building capability, what about negotiation capability, what about his capability to build inclusion and for creative deal-making? There have been many occasions when a customer has asked me to stand reference while looking for a new job.

Commercially win-win deals recognize the impossibility of predicting the future accurately. Unusual events happen all the time in a world that is in a state of great flux. Who can predict the next big natural disaster, terrorist act or stock-market meltdown? The world of business is no longer insulated from the environment. We all have to plan for contingencies, knowing that all contingencies cannot be planned for. This requires a certain flexibility on both sides that allows them to re-examine the assumptions on which an agreement rests. If that flexibility does not exist, one of the two sides invariably loses. Contractual unhappiness is infectious. Sooner rather than later, it affects both the sides. It is important therefore to build flexibility and rise above contractual terms in dealing with unusual situations that may arise.

Good sellers find good buyers and together, they build a virtuous cycle of sustainable growth. In today's world that power is formidable.

The lack of customer due diligence can mean a huge opportunity loss as everyone has limited bandwidth—only so much time and energy at disposal—in the world of business. If you get locked in with the wrong customer, watch out—your competition is becoming formidable because it is in business with the right one!

*

A few years back, I was invited to listen to Bill Gates speak at an invitation-only session in which a dozen IT entrepreneurs sat with great expectation at the Maurya Sheraton hotel in Delhi. I had never seen him live and to me it was close to seeing God. I had gone there with the expectation that after listening to him, I would have the clairvoyance to see into the future.

Bill Gates arrived, wished everyone and proceeded to explain in the course of his hour-long presentation as to how Windows would save the world. I was deeply disappointed. You do not expect a messiah to speak like a salesman. But here he was, the great technology guru, the richest geek on the planet—unabashedly selling what he makes!

Then sense dawned on me. If you cannot sell your own product, your sales executives cannot either. If you do not lead the way to bring business, don't expect them to do so. If you do not have pride in your own little thing, however ordinary it is, neither will the world. The no. 1 job of an entrepreneur is to sell his ware.

I come across countless highly competent technocrats who know how to make a gizmo but they do not like the act of selling. Yet, they yearn to start a company. My simple advice: don't. To start a company, you must love two things: selling your company and its products and the very concept of making money, as I have said before.

The reason I like telling the Bill Gates story is that you have to enjoy and lead the process of customer acquisition and retention. When Bill sells, everyone else follows suit. Bill's job is not to evangelize on the future. He is not God.

He is a businessman who loves his products and wants you to buy Windows.

When you start your own enterprise, never think that it is largely the sales person's job to sell. In today's world if you have a surrogate relationship with customers, the risk that they will switch loyalties will be much more. When salesmen leave, they take customers with them. When customers go, they can destroy your business.

*

The first few customer wins sometimes happen by providence. It has less to do with your great abilities as a salesman. An angel comes and gives you the business for reasons beyond what can be rationally explained. Of course, as you get bigger and you look back at the many subsequent wins, things fall in the realm of the explainable.

It is therefore important to accept the early wins with great humility and treasure them. The folklore about those wins and relationships must never die within the organization.

When you come to MindTree's Bangalore office, you will see our History Wall. Even if we are a young company, we capture historic moments that have defined our journey. There, you will see, exhibit number 1—the first invoice we raised on Lucent Technologies, for all of $49,000. It was our very first engagement in the US. Next to it, you can see a picture of our first customer in India—K. Ramesh of Hindustan Lever, the Unilever operation in India, who had endorsed MindTree when we had no track record, and no references worth the name.

I have a feeling that every company goes through three distinct phases before it settles into a virtuous cycle of customer relationships. There is something providential about each of these three phases.

In phase 1, you meet your angel customers. Irrespective of how deserving you are, they look at you kindly and let you have their business. Here, it is usually beginner's luck at work.

In phase 2, destiny tests you out—you are shown some lucrative choices that on scrutiny, you realize, you should not be making. This is the phase in which you might be tempted to do the right business with the wrong customer and even the wrong business with the right customer. If you choose to walk the middle ground and pass the test, you go on to phase 3, in which you settle into a routine in which you and the right kind of customers gravitate towards each other and a long virtuous cycle ensues.

In phase 2, often difficult choices must be made. You must know what business is not right for you and which customer will drag you down.

You must always give your best to the angel customers and keep going back to check if you could give them some more. In turn, do not just ask for money. Ask the angel if you could co-own rights on a product or service idea in lieu of a price reduction during the next cycle for contract renewal. Ask if the angel would address your employees on the occasion of your first anniversary. Ask if the angel would agree to speak to the press for you. Ask if the angel would endorse you to an analyst. Or if the angel would agree to be featured on your website, or would agree to give a customer reference, sit on your advisory board, endorse you to a second-round investor. Or any number of other things. Even advice on hiring a particular person for heading the sales function.

Ask and ask some more. But ask occasionally. Before that however, give, give and give in abundant measure.

MY THIRTY GOLDEN RULES FOR GETTING THE EARLY CUSTOMERS

1. Write to all your contacts from the past without an exception and without any expectations.
2. Build a prototype, actually keep building them all your life—show them off proudly to whoever comes your way. The world likes a toy.
3. Buy a database of prospective customers, send them a Power Point or a PDF document explaining what you do, not just an e-mail introduction.
4. Call on your larger competitor's installed client base in person—do not just push your products and services, ask if there is *anything* else you could do for them given your capability and willingness. Ask for a small opportunity, a pilot project.
5. Always ask your existing customers to give you new leads.
6. Always go back to people who disqualified you in a bidding round for some business you were competing for and update them on what is new and different at your end.
7. Keep your banker periodically posted on what you do, ask her for leads.

8. Visit trade shows regularly and talk to people at the exhibition stalls about what you do. Specially make it a point to attend vertically-focused, industry-specific trade shows.

9. Seek alliances with industry leaders—these are typically product and service companies that always need new partners to make their sale happen. Have someone exclusively focus on alliance building. Seek low-cost, co-branding opportunities for events along with them.

10. Become a member of the right industry bodies. Attend their events and seek opportunities for participation through speaking engagements in their seminars and conferences.

11. Write generic articles for the business press aligned to your area of work.

12. Regularly seek out industry analysts, brief them on your work, get some of them to visit you. They love tracking upcoming companies, so seek out a few analysts and personally focus on them over time.

13. Build a relationship with a few academic and research institutions, do some exploratory work with them, involve them with internal projects and events.

14. Co-locate your seniormost people in geographies where your customers are located. Some founders must be physically based where customers are.

15. Locate mutual opportunities with similarly situated, similarly sized companies.

16. Brief the commercial attachés of the embassies of countries with whom you want to establish a business relationship, invite them over. Though they are usually

focused on the established players, remember, everyone loves an underdog.

17. Track new investments coming up in various fields through venture funding and private equity. This is publicly available information. Write to them and follow up with a phone call.

18. Call on your investor's other investment companies, periodically nag your investor for a business lead. Do not feel disheartened if nothing comes up, though.

19. Call on your customer's suppliers and see who else they are selling to. Go along with them and make sales calls.

20. Have a great website with search optimization done so that website-generated leads can come in.

21. When hiring senior people, seek business leads. Be careful about their non-compete agreements with previous employers and do not get them to violate other people's intellectual property in the process. You can get sued.

22. Invite trade and educational delegations to visit your premises.

23. Speak to a few very large competitors and see if there is an alliance possibility.

24. Personally build a relationship with select journalists who track your industry.

25. Build a relationship with local government officials who promote your industry.

26. When a new sales person is appointed, go along with the person and make calls with her, discuss her rolodex and see if there is an opportunity.

27. Periodically attend learning conferences and network with speakers and attendees.

28. Do not fall into the Tender Loving Call (TLC) trap of repeatedly pitching to a sympathetic person who has no capability to give you any business but is always very nice to you. Save that energy and without fear of rejection, make real sales calls on wooden-faced, tough-talking prospects.

29. Speak to the person seated next to you—in an airplane, a business lounge, a dentist's waiting area or an industry event and ask him what he does.

30. Make cold calls, accompany your sales folks often and without being tired.

TWELVE

Managing Your Money

It is all about money. In business, more than anywhere else, it is apt to say this. After all, a business has to do with investments and revenues, expenses and taxes, depreciation and interest and profits. Having said that, this book is not a primer on financial accounting or business finance. One chapter is not enough to teach anyone how to manage money well. However, I do want to share with you a few points on the subject. Nothing very profound or magical, but a few useful tips, nevertheless. Pick a paragraph, contemplate the message, think for yourself and get more information from a professional on the subject.

First of all, to be an entrepreneur, you have to always remember four things.

You must love money. If the concept of generating wealth does not excite you, do not waste your time and that of others trying to build an enterprise.

Second, you must be excited about the generative power of wealth.

Third, you need to respect money so that you are able

to appreciate frugality and the importance of fiscal discipline.

Fourth, at the core of money management is the need for transparency and maintaining a record of all transactions.

After our very first meeting to contemplate entrepreneurship, co-founder Krishna Kumar and I called on Prof. N. Balasubramanian at the Indian Institute of Management. He was once the executive vice president, corporate finance, at Wipro. We needed to talk to someone like him about the idea of starting out on our own. Professor Balasubramanian listened to us patiently and gave us only two pieces of advice. One, he said, write down your idea in the form of a business plan. Two, always overestimate your costs and underestimate your revenues. Krishna Kumar and I took his words very seriously. I suggest you do too.

Writing down the business plan is not a one-time affair. In all of the six years at MindTree, every year starts with everyone writing down a business plan at a functional level that states the goals, objectives, strategy and investment needed at the department level. All these get rolled up to build an annual business plan that gets frozen as a month-wise and quarter-wise document. We share it with the board and then, with their comments, make a final plan that is shared with every MindTree Mind at the start of the fiscal year. Every quarter, we report progress on it. It is a discipline that is fundamental to building large organizations. So, start with a business plan and internalize the planning culture.

The next thing that we did right at MindTree was that the founders in the internal board agreed that we would not compensate ourselves at market rates.

I met a very senior, very well-paid executive of an

international company. He had started feeling bored with his successful career and was tempted to do something on his own. He asked me, 'I am so well taken care of. Tell me, how do I *extricate* myself.' I replied, 'You cannot.' It is important not to milk the budding enterprise just because one has led a life of extravagance as a salaried professional.

From the beginning, we put in place an auditable accounting system. Rostow Ravanan is a chartered accountant; he agreed to baby-sit the function till a full-time chief financial officer was brought in. Venkatesan K., a qualified accounts and finance manager, took charge of all day-to-day transactions. More importantly, the finance and account processes were designed meticulously, aimed at serving the needs of the larger organization but reporting directly to Ashok. In MindTree, the two functions that report directly to Ashok till date are finance and quality.

We also decided that we would hire the services of the best lawyers, the best accounting firms and the best auditors when it came to running the business. The *best* need not be the costliest. While initiating discussions, to each of these organizations we sold ourselves so that they saw us as more than just paying clients. In the process, they signed up for a long-term relationship and gave us their very best, whenever a need arose.

The role of the chief finance officer was kept open till Ashok was personally convinced that he had got the best person for the job. It wasn't going to be a compromise decision ever. While the head of finance must be good at budgeting, planning, cost and investment management and compliance, the person must also have one other ability:

that of being able to question the management without fear or favour.

Many start-ups maintain their accounts with spread-sheets for a long time. From the very beginning, we had an accounting package. That by itself is a non-trivial decision that pays back through the accountability and governance it helps to build. If your investors do not have confidence in your ability to close your books on demand or do not quite believe the accuracy of the numbers you generate, they will never give you the respect you deserve. You will see it in their dealings with you on a day-to-day basis. So, beware. Cut no corners here.

Respect your bean counters. Let the entire organization know that these folks are empowered by you. At the same time, fully involve them in business decision-making. Take them on sales calls with you once in a while and call them for gross margin discussions before you bid for that large deal. Do not seek submissive behaviour from them. If they are given to servile behaviour, they will not protect the financial interests of the organization. They will focus on pleasing you instead.

One of the most common reasons a start-up fails is that it runs out of money. So, do not lock money in things like land and building. Whatever you can hire, do not buy. Rather than block money in assets that attract depreciation and hence, depress your valuation, spend that money on appointing another sales person or adding five more delivery people. Similarly, do not rush into appointing another secretary or receptionist or such non-billable or non-customer facing people. Keep their number low—even try and keep that number constant in the initial growth period. After three years or so, that number as an overall percentage of the workforce should actually come down.

Add headcount only after people are running at 125 per cent of their capacities.

Do not hire full-time people in areas where you can 'rent' services.

Do not employ cooks and drivers and 'office boys' and gardeners and security guards on company payroll—even if they happen to be your wife's cousins, or your own. You will be surprised that this caution needs to be repeated even in today's day and age!

Know what must be measured in your business. In the services industry, it is about utilization, gross margins and outstandings as equal to number of days of sales. If you have a good hold on these, you know what to measure, what questions to ask. Every business has its own key parameters which indicate the health of the organization.

The critical thing about measurements is: circulate them to everyone and review them with religious regularity. Know what the best organizations in related and sometimes unrelated fields are measuring and what the competition is measuring.

When you bid for new work, calculate gross margin. If you must 'buy' business, do so after you have calculated the gross margin and have a data-driven decision-making culture in the organization.

Watch all outstanding receivables with a hawk's eye. Go after those that cross ninety days and breathe down people's necks for anything that remains uncollected beyond 180 days.

Build an asset-tracking system within the first ninety days of starting your company.

Do not pay salaries that cannot be justified to the customer. When you hire a new person, always look at the total cost of that person to the company. The ultimate cost of employing that individual is usually double of what you pay through the payroll. When you add up the office space, the accessories and the travel costs, it all adds up. So, build productivity expectations from every individual as a multiplier of that total cost.

Opening each new international office in a new geography costs a million dollars at the least. Each new vertical—or business line—you add in the software business costs at least $5 million before paying back.

No new sales person delivers in the first six months. However, if a sales person does not deliver in the first one year, he *never* will. Even if he is your first cousin.

Do not give away equity in lieu of space, advertising and other such facilities. Borrow and repay that investment if need be. If the value of your stock is not going to be several times higher than the interest on borrowing, then what is the point of building a business? By that logic, if the return is going to be several times more than what the bank would charge as interest, why pay for services with equity?

Write off capital investment using the most stringent accounting principle. At MindTree, we write-off all R&D expenses in the same year in which we incur the cost. We write off all software in year one and all desktop computers in two years.

A lot of bankers and investment experts will come by

and tell you to do financial engineering from time to time. They will sound like they are saints and angels and have no personal interest other than your well-being. Do not do things which promise to make you rich quick. Do not embrace schemes that defy conventional wisdom and plain common sense.

Do not do 'a little' accounting jugglery here and a little there, just because everyone else is doing it.

When an accounting practice becomes questionable in law, follow the law. If that hurts the business, take it up with an industry body and the government. Do not violate the law because it is uncomfortable to comply with it. Know that someone is just waiting for you to trip so that he can claim his pound of flesh in these matters.

Report your accounts to your investors on time, with zero window-dressing. Tell them all the uncomfortable stuff before they find it out and ask them for their advice on how to deal with the situation.

If you have multiple investors, remain apolitical. Irrespective of their quantum of funding, they must get the same financial information at the same time.

Run your board meetings on time, with pre circulated agenda and published data. During the board meeting, pretend that you are a Fortune 500 company listed on NASDAQ or the New York Stock Exchange. Your business decisions, your transparency will be closely followed by the market, hence building a disciplined approach from the very start will prepare you well for the time when you are a public company.

In the first, partial year of operation, we clocked less

than $1 million. Six years after that, we clocked over $102 million. Throughout the years the fervour of our board meetings remained the same, quite irrespective of the size. Ashok settles the dates for the once-a-quarter board meeting a year in advance. The dates seldom change. During the four hours of intense meeting, there is an air of formality and seriousness that transforms us completely. Even though we have great personal rapport and friendship with people on the board at a personal level, when the meeting commences, these are left outside the door. Our investors love us for that.

Let us peep into a typical MindTree board meeting and look at what we do.

Every review begins with a look at the balance sheet and the cash flow—the sources of money inflow, the heads of expenses and the net flow—for the last one quarter. In running any business, cash flow is very important. Sometimes, it is more important than even profitability.

Then we look at the overall financial performance of the last quarter and the trend for the next quarter. We look at how the quarter has grown year-on-year and quarter-on-quarter for the company as a whole and then for the individual businesses we are in. As you grow and begin different lines of businesses, make sure to track them individually. No major line of business should get hidden in the overall numbers; it must be presented by itself.

We look at how the quarter has done against the annual plan. Many businesses have a predictable rhythm. For example, in a service business, if you do not have an order pipeline healthy enough in the first two quarters, it is unlikely that you will meet your annual numbers.

Then we look at a few operational performance indices. These include the data on customer addition—how many are active and how many are new.

We track the customer dependency—what share of business do the top five customers have—and we discuss how to bring that dependency down.

We then look at the accounts receivables as days of outstanding and ageing of the receivable.

We look at the business-wise and geography-wise revenue split and ask questions about why things are the way they are.

We focus on the utilization trend in the organization. We do so by looking at all major lines of business.

We focus on how our investments are doing. This refers to extra cash sitting in the bank, including investor capital. As a principle, we do not put these into risky, high-interest instruments ever. Our job is to make money in our chosen line of business, we are not a foreign exchange speculator or a stock-market player. It is never a good idea to put the extra cash in speculative transactions.

We look at people numbers and thoroughly analyse two things: attrition and percentage of non-billable people to billable people. If you can remain below industry level in both, you know that you are doing all right.

We also look at capital expenditure. It is always pre-approved. And as I said before, we do not invest in capital expenditure if it can be brought in as a revenue item. The problem of all capital expenditure is that it attracts depreciation. When you depreciate your assets, your profitability goes down. When your profitability goes down, your valuation is less. In a start-up, valuation is very important at all times.

Then we look at billing rates and ask why these are the way they are. We compare them with leading players. We ask ourselves how billing rates could improve.

Into the fifth year of our existence, we introduced a new set of review points. These are a qualitative summary of what went well and what did not. These points cover the business as a whole and then are used to evaluate all major functions within the organization.

We look at four sets of key ratios: those relating to the balance sheet, a whole bunch of ratios relative to growth, profitability ratios at gross margin, Earnings Before Interest, Tax, Depreciation and Amortization (EBITDA) and Profit Before Tax (PBT) as a percentage of sales, and lastly, the ratio of billable versus non-billable people.

In summary, entrepreneurs must understand fiscal management well. There are many courses available in leading management schools that teach you functional basics. Once you understand those, try and see them at work in whatever organization you currently work in. Go beyond the call of your regular work and learn about how the business of business works. Read the balance sheets of a few leading public companies, read a financial newspaper and at least one business periodical with regularity. All these will progressively equip you to run your business as a financial success some day.

THIRTEEN

Building Your Brand

Just as you must understand the fundamentals of money, you must also understand the fundamentals of how brands are built, because a brand is often all you leave behind. Products change, services change, methodologies, processes, tools, people—everything changes, but it is the brand that lives on to attract customers, employees and suppliers over time and help create value. What is a brand?

A brand is the communication of your inner worth over a period of time. It builds up into a shared understanding of who you are, what you stand for. It attracts people to your products and services so that they become loyal customers, and it is the factor that makes others want to work with you as their preferred employer.

Many of us think a brand is all about advertising. First of all, building a brand is not equal to advertising. Brands need communication of their values. Advertising is just one of the many, and often the most expensive and least remunerative, avenues of doing so.

Building a brand is something that must be thought-out well, led by top management and woven into every single aspect of the organization's working. Only then, can one build a great brand. Yet, till you begin to benefit from it, it remains an intangible, abstract thing. Let us try to understand the brand mystique a little more.

Building a brand begins with deciding the DNA, the mission, the vision and the values of the organization. Thereafter, day after day, the organization has to live these and in the process, create discernible value. Brand projection must be consistent with these.

There a few critical things we must keep in mind while branding the organization. One is choosing the name itself. The other is in choosing the visual identity of the organization. It is a good idea to take the help of a brand expert, as against an advertising agency, while deciding these.

In the case of MindTree, while choosing a name (see story under the culture section on www.mindtree.com) we hired a company in California called NameIt.

We shared with them our mission, vision, values and our broad business plan. They suggested a few hundred names that would appropriately describe the company we wanted to create and from these, we chose MindTree.

While choosing a name, attention must be paid to its uniqueness. Unless it is a coined name, as against a word in the dictionary, getting a trademark registration becomes an issue. One needs to pay attention to other aspects as well, like how memorable it is, its cultural scalability—its ability to convey the same meaning across various cultural contexts—and its availability as an Internet domain name. If you choose a name that is already taken as an Internet domain, you would have to buy the latter out, otherwise each time people click on your domain name, you lose the brand value of the name of the company itself. A name may work well in one language or country and be a complete no-no in another. Finally, a name must evoke positive subliminal feelings. Sometimes, people modify the names of existing, successful players and create variants from them. It is hardly the sign of a leader and while in personal life, it may be a done thing to choose the name of a celebrity for your child, it does not help while doing so for your organization. After choosing a name, some people start abbreviating it and the abbreviation begins to get a life of its own. Remember, each time someone uses the abbreviated name in a document or a conversation, the real name is lost and there goes your brand recall.

Sometimes great names are picked up just like that and become great brands—Apple and Google are good examples of that. It does not, however, mean that a name is just a name. The right name provides a great opportunity to begin the branding process well—choosing a name with care certainly helps.

Then comes the visual representation or the logo. The Singapore Airlines logo reminds me of the garuda, the strongest of all birds and the chosen carrier of the gods. The Lufthansa crane is symbolic of many good things in many different cultures. Among its attributes is the ability to fly long distances across land and sea. The Apple logo, with a piece bitten off, is a great temptation. The Nike swoosh is revolutionary and indicates speed. The Mercedes-Benz logo is about engineering perfection.

I am not going to tell you how to create or choose a

visual design for yourself. It is an involved subject in itself. All I am telling you here is that it is an important issue and paying attention to it will help create a great brand. The logo or the visual representation of your brand is a graphic symbol, with or without the name of the organization. Again, while looking at it, consider its appeal to your constituents, its ability to evoke positive feelings that convey the DNA and the mission of the company. You need to look at how easy or difficult it will be to reproduce across different media, including depiction over the Internet. How will it look on poor quality newsprint, sweatshirts and small give-aways to large billboards on the Ginza in Tokyo. It does not hurt to look into every small detail.

Once you have got your name and logo right, think about your positioning. This is to determine how differently you would be perceived from your competition. It is based on differentiation that we have talked about in chapter 6. It is basically a visually explainable diagram that shows where you stand vis-à-vis other players. In the beginning, it may be an aspirational view but over time, you have to live with the positioning statement you make. As you grow the positioning may have to change because of environmental factors such as customer needs and an altered competitive landscape. It may also change based on internal factors like new products and services or way of doing things.

When we started in 1999, the positioning as a high consulting–lower cost company—that is, providing high consulting capability at a lower cost when compared to international players—gave us immediate response. Over time, without losing that virtue, we had to embrace the positioning of being the best mid-size company out of India in the IT services space. This was a response to the traction of large organizations like Volvo and AIG and Burger King and IATA who wanted to deal with a company our size. They perceived that being very large, some of our competitors could not deliver them access, attention and agility. Sometimes, positioning ideas emerge from customer responses such as this.

Following the positioning, it is a good idea to create what is called a 'message map'. A message map helps to deliver a consistent message across the organization while dealing with many external constituents. A message map is not a bunch of nice-sounding words but a clear statement of what the organization is all about. It is directly related to the values the organization brings to the table. As with positioning, the message map needs to be revisited from time to time. The purpose of the message map is not to make everyone say the same thing but to ensure that in all external communications, the key messages get delivered. (See box for our early message map around the year 2000.) A message map is not a brochure or a hand-out. It contains key message points, elicits interested questions from the listener and gives you a chance to drive home points you want the listener to remember about you. For each statement in the box, you would expect a response like 'Tell me how or give me an example.' That helps to drive a good conversation on the organization you are trying to build. I would never go to an analyst meeting or a press-briefing without looking at the message map and rehearsing a few things in my mind.

EARLY MESSAGE MAP OF MINDTREE
AROUND YEAR 2000

MindTree Consulting delivers affordable business solutions through global software development. Affordability is becoming a major issue for companies. On the one hand you have US-based consulting companies that cost you an arm and a leg. These companies do not scale. On the other hand, there have been 'offshore' companies that do not have a business-backward view, consulting skills or project-management capabilities. We formed MindTree Consulting in 1999 to be able to bring affordability to businesses by creating a global model that delivers the best of both.

We organize ourselves as the IT services and the R&D service business.

On the IT services side, we design applications to help businesses succeed using IT for

Web Applications, ERP deployment, Supply Chain Management and Mobility Applications. Our customers are companies like Avis, Franklin Templeton, Hindustan Lever, Lucent Technologies, Prudential and Sun.

On the R&D services side, we create embedded software for building next generation network equipment that involves 3G, WAP, Bluetooth and VOIP. Our customers include companies like Alcatel, Atoga, Cisco, Hitachi.

To deliver affordable business solutions, our vision is to build a truly global company. We started off with a global management team that commands confidence. We have built large, successful companies before. Our founding team came from companies like Wipro,

Cambridge Technology Partners and Lucent. The ten founders belong to three nationalities.

We raised money globally. Our first-round funding of $9.5 million was from Walden, a $1.3 billion US-based venture fund, and Global Technology Ventures, an Indian venture fund. Our second-round funding that is just over raised us an additional $14.4 million—this round was led by the Capital Group of the US.

From day 1, we were genetically engineered to be global. In two years, we have gone from 0 to 450 people from ten different national origins in three continents.

Our current business success validates our vision. We have globally delivered seventy-five projects so far. Our year one revenue of $15 million was ahead of our commitment to our VCs. We are looking at growth rates significantly ahead of the industry year after year and will be a $231 million company by 2005. In less than two years, we have offices in US, UK, India, Singapore and Japan.

We are raising the bar for global development by collapsing time zones, geographies and costs. We have an 'always on' model. For companies like iSpheres, Oakland, we have a development team that never sleeps. Working shoulder to shoulder with their in-house team, we are helping this software maker beat time and cost through a team that is partly in the US and partly in India. At iSpheres, we are co-developing mission critical, leading edge software for supply chain applications.

We are helping Franklin Templeton re-architect their thirty-seven different websites to one Global Website Project that involves more than three dozen people in the

US and India. It is a state-of-the-art project that involves interacting with business users, architecture design and, finally, development using a 24*7 model.

Our Global Development Model is helping companies like iSpheres, Avis and Franklin and Hitachi to realize projects at 40 to 50 per cent less than what US-based leading consulting companies can deliver. This is happening because of our ability to create a 'one shore' pricing model that appropriately dips into a global talent pool that is highly connected.

What do all these mean to our customers? To them, we are able to deliver predictable business outcomes. Predictable business outcome means four things. We take a 360-degree view of their business. We deliver dramatic cost reduction through ahead-of-time work done at MindTree Labs. We have formalized processes that create a white-box-view of the development process. Finally, we look for clear business justification. If it does not make money for our clients, it does not make sense to us.

People commend us for our global development model. Yet they worry about how long it will be before the best companies in the US and in India will try and emulate us. Well, they certainly have woken up to what we envisioned three years back. Many companies are trying to be global by migrating one way or the other. We were genetically engineered to be global. In our business, the biggest barrier to entry is culture. At MindTree, we are building a culture of empathy. It has two aspects to it. Externally, we sense our customer's pain and we make sure that we look at 'relationships' and not 'transactions'.

Internally, we base our company culture through our

DNA of Imagination, Action and Joy. On top of this, we are building our value system that we call CLASS. Caring. Learning. Achieving. Sharing. And, Social Sensitivity. That broadly tells you who we are.

Having spoken about positioning and the message map, we should shift the conversation to two other things: your intranet and your website.

Your intranet site is more than just a nice looking thing. In time, it will become your most important communication real estate. I like to look at an intranet site as what I call a 'salt lick'. In forests, different animals may graze or hunt all over the forest, but periodically, they must all come to the salt lick from where they take back vital salt. In forests that do not have natural sources of sodium, conservationists create salt licks for the animals. The intranet is your organizational salt lick. That is where people keep coming back. So, you must pay attention to not only the look and feel (consistent with your brand) of the structure but most importantly, the content. Content is like fish. Make sure, it is always delivered fresh. Richer the content of the intranet and higher the built-in interactivity, greater will be your capacity to create instant communication and a feedback system.

Now, let us talk about your website. In the electronic age, the website has become the most important marketing tool for any enterprise. It is the face of the organization. In many instances, it is also the gateway to doing business. It is very different from any traditional communication platform because it is always 'on', you have no control over who comes to it, and it lends itself to search parameters, that is, people can search for selective information, and thereby it gives you the power to deliver finely honed messages. Anyone you make an employment offer to, or anyone who considers you for any business, will first come to your site and form his or her impressions.

Once again, the website must flow from your DNA, your mission, vision and values. The quality of in-house generated content, the kind of things it gives away to a visitor as 'downloads', the sense of inclusion it creates and the interactivity it can generate, determine the usefulness of a website. It is not a 'do it once and use forever' kind of thing. Periodically, you must look at your and your competitor's website, listen to feedback from outsiders and focus on fresh, useful content. Give some thought to search engine optimization. If someone does a Google search with a word that can be a lead-in, invest some time and money to ensure that your company name pops up against it.

At some stage in your life, probably in year two, think of hiring a good public relations (PR) agency. Most start-ups do not need a huge advertising effort to begin with. What they do need is delivery of very thinly sliced messages to a carefully chosen target audience like the trade press, market analysts and opinion leaders. You can build a relationship with them through a good PR agency.

When you choose a PR agency, sell yourself to them, induct them into your company the same way you would induct a senior colleague. Then ask them to help you create a message map and train you in media handling. You will thank me for this piece of advice.

While working with PR agencies, make sure you draw a PR plan and generate enough content and events such that they are able to position your organization and spread the word about new achievements and developments. However, they cannot position you on the basis of what you are not. Hence perceptible value, and not fluff, must precede any PR exercise.

Get trained on how to handle the press. Never, ever say anything untrue to the press. In interacting with journalists, know that there is no such thing as off the record. Pre-discuss issues with investors before going to the press if it could impact them in any way. That rule applies even more to your customers. They do not like to be surprised by reading their name in the press and most of them are very sensitive about your using their name or logo. It is always a good idea to seek permission first, seeking forgiveness later usually does not work well.

Look for speaking opportunities in trade and industry forums, at leading educational institutions and customer events. These are very useful.

Encourage your senior people to write articles in your line of business in trade papers—it is worth its weight in gold. When you have published content, speeches and Power Point slides, put them up on your website. Content is a very powerful thing and develops a life of its own. In 2002, I was invited to deliver the commencement speech at the Indian Institute of Management at Bangalore. The speech, titled 'Go, Kiss the World', apparently struck a chord with people. It was circulated among thousands of people across the world, got published in dozens of in-house magazines, was carried in full by two national newspapers in India. Finally, it got reproduced by *Reader's Digest*—a good three years after I had delivered it. This excludes the hundreds of blogs that still keep it alive—so much so that a Google key-word search of 'Go, Kiss the World' picks up the speech I delivered a long time back. That is the power of content, thanks to the Internet.

Good content is a great way to brand the organization. While people spend a lot of time on creating communication platforms, they seldom realize that more the useful content a start-up can generate, greater is the chance of its name becoming memorable. Ask your people to write articles on the work they do, ask them to develop point of view documents, write make-believe interviews, write down experiences drawn from projects and development of products. Write, write and write some more. As I said earlier, content is like fish. Deliver it fresh and populate your website with it, all the time.

While on the subject of branding, think of the workplace as a great branding opportunity. All MindTree offices are awash with the colourful paintings of the children of the Spastic Society of Karnataka. Their work reinforces our DNA and our values. Our offices have a rare character you do not see elsewhere—any visitor who comes to see us, goes back deeply impressed with our inner core. It occurs to me that many entrepreneurs do not see the huge branding opportunity at the workplace. Workplace design and the brand identity can be beautifully intertwined. (See box at the end of the chapter, 'MindTree's West Campus'.)

Pay attention to the corporate presentation. Nominate a

senior person who is the 'keeper' of the corporate presentation. In MindTree, for the last six years, we have Scott Staples, co-founder and executive vice president, North America, who has been the keeper. He releases usually three updates every year and the look and feel as well as the content are consistent across the world. This makes a huge difference.

Early on in the life of the organization, get a design shop to freeze a corporate identity manual. It should address all issues of corporate design, from the font to the colours to the way the logo may or may not be used. It should be a living document that gets revised, but very occasionally. At MindTree, we have made no major revisions in six years.

Invest in a contact management system for the sales force. As you grow, you will lose the most vital aspect of your business: the trail of prospect and customer contacts people made—who met whom, what was discussed and how was the call closed? In MindTree, Joseph King, senior VP of marketing, insisted that all sales calls be recorded on a tool called Goldmine. It has been a great decision. As people change assignments and even prospects and customers change jobs, it is critical that the organization does not lose the continuity and a wealth of information that goes with it. Sometimes, the tool truly lives up to its name. Here is a story.

Many years back, someone from MindTree had called on an AIG official who said they were not looking for an IT partner and also that MindTree was too small. He said that in a year's time, AIG probably would open the door for vendor empanelment. All in all, not a productive call. Just so you know, AIG is the no. 1 insurance company of the US and its second largest financial services company. A year after, a new sales person named Ashutosh Shukla was running through Goldmine to see which all prospects were contacted in his territory over time and his eyes fell on AIG. He made an e-mail contact with the same person to say 'Happy new year'. What followed is the successful empanelment of MindTree and a multi-year, multi-million-dollar relationship. In most companies, the information on the first contact would have gone into a black hole. Invest in a sales tool and a contact management system as soon as you can.

People frequently ask me, what should be the marketing spend to build a great brand? It is a very difficult question to answer and depends on the type of business you are in, the kind of noise level created by the competitors, the business goals you have in mind and so on. There is no silver bullet, nor does one size fit all.

A good thing to do is to look at what the big players are doing and what the small players are doing. Who is doing smart things without spending a lot of money? Remember that it is very easy to spend money on advertising without any tangible success. The start-up years must be about building value, investing in getting reference-able customers and creating a soft buzz, rather than writing fat cheques for media advertising. Just so you know, at MindTree (again, not to generalize) in our sixth year, with a business at $100 million, our total marketing spend was half a million dollars. Advertising was a very small part of that.

If you are a product company, you may be required to

spend significantly more. The point, however, is to explore how one can conserve cash, look at alternative communication channels, spend more on building direct marketing, use the Internet, keep the media and market analysts continuously informed—than fall prey to an advertising agency that convinces you how print or television is the best way to spend investor money.

In building a brand, you will work with myriad agencies—your PR agency, advertising agency, a web development and content company and many others. Treat them all as you would treat your own people. Take them into confidence. Do not just tell them what you want them to do for you—tell them what your pain points are. You will be amazed how little start-ups understand the power of leverage and how much they underestimate the fact that many people like to do things for a start-up more than for an established identity. The way to unlock that energy is to treat people with inclusion.

Do not invest in building a brand before you are ready to serve a new geography. As a young company, it is important to have your feet on the ground and build capability to credibly handle inquiries first.

MINDTREE'S WEST CAMPUS : THE WORKPLACE AS BRAND AMBASSADOR

A note created in 2004 when the first phase of the campus was opened for activity.

MindTree's West Campus is located as part of the Global Village Technology Park on Mysore Road, Bangalore. It is a three-module design, to be completed in phases as we grow. When fully occupied, it will be capable of housing 5000 engineers. We have completed phase I, which is open for dedication now.

The three modules have been designed by RSP, a renowned international architectural firm, based on the theme of MindTree's DNA: Imagination, Action and Joy.

As you stand in front of the building, you will be greeted by a 'living logo'. It is a blue-and-red structure through which a living tree will grow. When in full bloom, the tree will add the yellow, thereby completing the colours of MindTree. This is a concept that, to the best of our knowledge, has never been done before.

At the base of the living logo, we will pour earth from the many countries to which MindTree Minds have gone to build value for our customers. Portions of the same earth are preserved inside the building in an exhibit called OneShore. Each time we go to newer lands, we will return with a handful of earth and pour it at the base of the living logo, as well as add some to the OneShore exhibit.

When you enter the foyer, you will see a metal tree in the reception area. All movements beyond this point require a MindTree badge, and the entire facility is monitored by security devices for the safety of MindTree's customers and MindTree Minds.

The building has all of 176,000 square feet of built-up area. While conceptualizing the design, we had a brief consisting of three things:

—The facility had to ensure memetic continuity with MindTree's past, particularly its work with specially-able people, like children with cerebral palsy, thereby continuing a tradition of social sensitivity and a business built on values.

—The facility had to be aspirational. We felt that the modern workplace does not become adequately aspirational from the personal standpoint of the knowledge worker. It does not inspire her to grow and become 'somebody'.

—The facility had to be delivered in a cost-effective manner.

The brief was made to a shortlist of four leading architecture firms. We finally chose to go with Chandavarkar and Thacker. Prem Chandavarkar won the assignment with his concept of fractal geometry in the design of leaves and growth pattern of trees. Several innovations have been made as a result.

The workplace is not a sea of workstations as you see in a typical software facility. Prem's study indicated that a typical work group consists of seven people. This happens to be the number of an average immediate family for most people. Groups of such families create a village. This corresponds to a typical large project or a development centre. Each village has a common congregation space called the Agora, a concept derived from the way the Greeks planned their habitats.

The Agora is a place to congregate, discuss issues or just hang out. Created with informal stone seating in Jaisalmer yellow, the Agora has a symbolic banyan tree structure in the centre with a number of white writing surfaces around it. It is a unique design concept that has not been tried anywhere else in the world.

Every conference room in the facility is state-of-the-art in regard to sound, conferencing and projection facilities, and is named after a unique tree in the world, either living or mythological. For example, you will see names like the Lone Cypress and the Bodhi as unique identifiers with a narrative for each.

Each floor has a History Wall that will be decorated with objects, designs and other memorabilia of the people who live on that floor. There is also a quiet room called the Still Mind for meditative silence.

On the ground floor, behind the reception, is the Rain Forest. It has a 200-seater, state-of-the-art dialogue room called the Kalpavriksha. Behind the Kalpavriksha are two learning rooms, each capable of handling forty-five learners. After these, you will find the Arboretum—this is where we will provide a special area in which we will assimilate 'lateral' (meaning experienced) new Minds because they are like grown-up trees getting uprooted to join MindTree, and being grown-up trees, they require special handling. The Arboretum is specially equipped to handle their needs, and includes a fifty-DVD set brought from Stanford University on subjects as varied as leadership and innovation.

Surrounding the Rain Forest is the History Wall and the Hero's Wall. The History Wall provides us with memetic continuity (memes are replicable ideas—a living organization is called a memeplex, a group of ideas). Hence, for a rapidly expanding organization, memetic continuity has to be planned such that growth does not become inherently destructive of values. On the History Wall, we have graphically presented our CLASS values with a superimposition of the first five years of MindTree as it became the first Indian company to reach 2000 people, the world's youngest P-CMM Level 5 and an SEI CMMi Level 5 company in just five years. The photographs and artefacts reflect the journey of the only company that has made it to all the three nationwide surveys for Best Employers: the Dataquest list, the Hewitt list and the Great Places to Work List of Best Employers.

The Hero's Wall reflects who all MindTree Minds want to grow up to be like. It celebrates personal excellence. We find that the typical software engineer does not want to work in an anthill but wants the workplace to be aspirational and inspirational. MindTree Minds were polled to find out who reflects this need among people past and living. Some of the most admired personalities have been presented on the Hero's Wall. This is meant to be a work in progress and each new facility will feature newer faces that will inspire MindTree Minds to grow in their own right.

The design story will be incomplete without pointing out the work of children with cerebral palsy. The entire facility is replete with their work—digitally expanded— that fills our consciousness in the same way that Chetan's logo of MindTree did, when we went to the Spastic Society of Karnataka's school at Bangalore in 1999, in search of our visual identity.

The graphic concepts were created in active collaboration with the Srishti School at Bangalore in a unique partnership between MindTree, Chandavarkar & Thacker, and Srishti students and faculty there. Arvind, a young design student, was 'embedded' as a MindTree Mind for months with MindTree's young engineers to soak in their desires, their hopes, their work and lifestyle. Srishti then went to the design board and created the ambience for the place.

Special attention was paid to workplace safety and ergonomics. Current designs of tables and chairs were changed with inputs from Dr B.R. Chaitanya, who got special customizable tables and chairs that will be safe and not expose our people to repetitive stress injury.

The facility is also equipped with MindTree's unique concept called 'Baby's Day Out'—a place to which young parents can bring their children when the crèche is closed, or there is a problem with the support system at home.

At the top of the terrace is the Palm Breeze cafeteria. It is a meeting place for MindTree Minds, who can lounge about with a view of the verdant skyline full of swaying coconut palms, overlooking, at a distance, a clubhouse, a golf course and the soon to be constructed Food Court by Tanglin Developers, who have created the 140-acre Global Village campus.

Around the 12-acre space in which MindTree is located, network-enabled open seating spaces for breakout sessions are coming up that provide relief from the glass-encased work areas. Also coming up is a driver's rest area, which will have full recreational and learning tools, and Internet connectivity for the car drivers who bring our guests to MindTree's West Campus and have to just wait while the guests spend time with us.

The West Campus will be a plastic-free space—we will not use any plastic material that is not reusable. The campus has several points at which rainwater will be harvested and sent to charge the underground water reserves.

All in all, the West Campus symbolizes the DNA of MindTree: Imagination, Action and Joy. In every small detail, it reflects the values of Caring, Learning, Achieving, Sharing and Social Sensitivity (CLASS) that bind MindTree Minds together.

FOURTEEN

Emergence and the Willingness to Change

A company is like a river. At its source, it gives you no indication of what it will eventually look like at its confluence. An entrepreneur must have that sagacious vision to be able to undertake the journey from the source—all the way to where the river meets the ocean.

As the river flows, it takes in many tributaries, changes course when faced with a difficult obstacle, falls and cascades, sometimes dries up and even goes underground before it meets the sea. Along the journey, it remains faithful to whoever comes to it. It builds a beneficial relationship with life around it. And keeps on with the journey.

Unlike a river, a rivulet may dry up every so often. Many entrepreneurs lose their way and dry up like a rivulet, unable to regenerate themselves, sometimes, confusing the path with the journey. The journey is both about steady vision and a willingness to change course.

It is strange but true—while conviction in a given vision

is critical for the entrepreneur, quite often, it is the same conviction that comes in the way of embracing change. It is like walking a tightrope—there is no one science, nor art to deciding when to stay the ground and when to abandon it. Yet, it is important that every entrepreneur understand two things. There is a systemic reality in which everything is connected. Something seemingly remote can often have unimaginable and rapid impact on a well-thought-out plan.

A bird flu in Hunan province that reaches Europe and threatens to mutate—could it impact the valuation of a high technology start-up in California? You bet it could. If the virus were to mutate, it would impact life and hence, business. If people cannot travel because of a pandemic, it has cascading economic impact. That in turn could hurt the stock market, and when the stock market is jittery for any prolonged period, venture capitalists become extra cautious.

A systemic view is useful because it helps us to go beyond a simple 'cause-effect' relationship of events. It also helps us to stay the course during both good times and bad times. Either one, for an entrepreneur, is a phase, and he must take the long-term view of things. When we build a systemic view of things, it helps us to appreciate the big picture, it helps us to know about the interconnected nature of things and, finally, we begin to understand the power of emergence.

What is emergence? Simply put, things unfold. We need to be perceptive about the process of unfolding and while embracing the inevitable, try and not be overawed by the changes around us. It also means that we have to sometimes go with the flow, sometimes against it, and sometimes stay ahead of it.

Start-up companies must know how to ride the surf, lest they are drowned by what can sometimes be unimaginable change.

However powerful the original vision behind the organization, no one exactly knows the future.

Did Steve Jobs know about Nano when he designed Apple IIe? Did Hewlett and Packard know that one day HP would be in the laser printer business? Did Azim Premji know as late as 1990 that he would be in the software services business? Did automobile executives in the US and Japan know that China and India, and not the US and Europe, would be their most important market—as late as the year 2000?

The story goes that sometime in the 1980s, the Infosys founders were up against a wall, unable to meet expenses. Some of the founders felt that the future simply did not exist and they were better off winding up and going their own ways. A heated debate ensued. Chairman Narayana Murthy stood his ground about persisting and offered to buy up the shares of the ones who felt unsure. The truth was that even he did not have money to pay for the shares at that time. Finally, they all cooled down and decided to stay put and went on to create a very valuable organization.

In 1993, the team took Infosys public. Its maiden IPO was undersubscribed when Infosys offered its shares at Rs. 95 apiece. These were shares with a face value of Rs. 10 at a premium of Rs. 85 per share. Who knew that the value of that one share worth Rs. 95 would in 2006 be worth Rs. 1,90,700—at a going market price of Rs. 2980 a share! Infosys is a great example of making emergence work.

The management of Infosys has an intuitive feel for the phenomenon.

The unpredictable nature of things has begun engaging management experts and professionals alike and we all know about contingency plans and anticipative management. In today's world, despite such tools being available, it is still not possible to fully predict both their positive and negative influences on business. So, on the one hand, we need to accept discontinuities caused by such unpredictable events and not be in denial. On the other hand, we need to look for the opportunities that such events invariably create. In all this, we have to make sense of what is going on, respond to the changes and at the same time, budget time and energy to help the organization to cope with changes. We have to go to our people and tell them why things are the way they are. We have to explain the larger scheme of things and where the organization fits in, where it needs to calibrate itself and when it has to morph.

When we started MindTree, it was focused on the Internet and the telecom domains. Both came to a standstill soon after. Meanwhile, our key customers—Unilever and Volvo—wanted us to understand supply chain- and mainframe-based applications respectively. The market had changed dramatically. Post-9/11, all new software development just stalled. There was money only in re-engineering and maintenance projects. We were not a company that had any competence in these areas—we had to learn that stuff. On the R&D services side of the house, we had to keep several areas of IP development on the backburner and learn altogether new areas to be able to survive.

I remember how our storage area capability was developed during this time. We knew nothing in this area. We learnt from the indications that this was going to be big. Since we had no capability, how could we make an entry?

One of our leaders, Ananda Rao Ladi, went to attend a trade show in San Francisco. He came back and built something called Internet Small Computer System Interface (iSCSI) Simulator. It was like a proof-of-concept. He took it to potential customers, showing it to them whether they needed it or not. Some would say, leave it behind. Others, if MindTree could build that, why can we not get them to build something related? Some would simply throw him out. But over time, that iSCSI Simulator expertise became a huge door opener. One thing led to another.

Today, we have very solid experience in that area and are considered to be a significant technology source. Ananda's going around the trade show and thereafter following the path of emergence is a great example of being a path creator. In the process, many times, you also need to give up an established path.

Be emergent with customers and employees. At the same time, do not jump into what your competitors are doing without a due thought process. You do not always fully understand what is in their minds. After we started MindTree, everyone jumped into the world of Business Process Outsourcing (BPO). They were deeply convinced that this would be the next big thing. We stayed away from it. Our take was quite straightforward. Every diversification takes up top management energy. The top team has finite energy and must focus and deliver on what it knows best before straying into unrelated areas. We have always maintained that every business is complex. Just because someone says something is very simple, never believe it. At high volumes, if you care about doing a job really well, even cleaning toilets is a complex business. It becomes management intensive. So, be careful.

The power of emergence, harnessed well, can lead to unusual discoveries and innovations. For this, one has to give people and partners porous boundaries such that they develop their own ideas and come up with alternatives rather than telling them what exactly to do in every given situation. When we built a half-million-square-foot new facility off Bangalore, we called in Prem Chandavarkar, a leading architect, we got students of a local design school called Srishti, the children of the Spastic Society of Karnataka and an in-house team and asked them to conceive a next-generation workplace. The starting point was to explore many possibilities, move from one semi-finished idea to another till we had on our hands an outstanding creation. As a process, this is very different from calling people in and telling them what to do.

Emergence is about comfort with the process of exploration and an inner conviction that it would eventually lead to a higher level of progress.

Sometimes, that process can lead you into making serious mistakes. Two things are critical—the willingness to let people make those mistakes and creating an atmosphere in which people feel secure in discussing their mistakes. Early in our lives, we had to write off a couple of million dollars for wrong business moves. If MindTree were a centralized organization, we would probably not have made those mistakes. Yet, we were clear that we were here to seek a rapid growth company that would be led by many people. The only way you could make that happen was to let them take local decisions, and some invariably would bomb. Ashok was supremely at peace when some of them did indeed go wrong—he never ever goes back to rake up the past. The result? We have one of the finest middle management teams in the industry.

Emergence is also about not taking hard positions when issues emerge, unless they involve a fundamental business principle or values. Sometimes, you will encounter very demanding, very difficult business issues. While negotiating, many times a new entrepreneur gets boxed in. In encountering a tough situation, you may sometimes want to believe:

— There are *only two* possible outcomes of this conversation—a 'yes' or a 'no'
— I *have* to take a decision in the matter *right now*
— I have to agree or disagree with the proposal, right *this* moment
— Only *I can* solve the problem on hand.

None of the above may be true. You may have choices you do not know because you have closed your mind by getting boxed into a certain way of thinking. One thing to keep in mind—actively create sounding boards. It is a good idea to have different sounding boards for different kinds of situations. Do not lock yourself in with just one mentor or confidante who is expected to know everything. Early in the game, identify someone who is good on relationship issues, someone good in matters of finance and someone good at business issues. These people should have your complete trust so you can talk to them. Sometimes, a second opinion helps.

When you have no one to talk to and the matter involves your customer, share your issues with your customer, explain your constraints and ask him or her for advice or to collaborate with you to strategize the outcome. You have nothing to lose.

Emergence is about instituting a strong culture of discussions and active disagreement. Sometimes people seek too much of alignment—too often we want to rush into a fast-forward mode to the best decision possible. There is no such thing as the 'best decision'. In most matters, you will find out, one thing leads to another. The definitive end-state or the perfect decision is elusive and mostly non-existent. Given that, encourage people to not only debate all important issues, but to disagree with each other.

If you have not yet read Edward de Bono's *Six Thinking Hats*, you should do so. Learn to wear different hats at different times so that you will be open to viewpoints and alternative paths.

Sometimes, you will be told that the *only* way to save a deal is to agree to a 'build-own-operate-transfer' model. Or, the *only* way to retain your people is to agree to an across-the-board 20 per cent hike in salaries or give away some more stocks right away. Or, the *only* way to fend off competition is to get bought over. Question them every time someone utters these two words: *only way*. There is no such thing.

In the initial years, you will meet a lot of self-styled advisers. Listen to everyone. But form your own opinion about things. Whenever someone tells you that the world is coming to an end soon or that there will be happy times ever after—show him the door. Nothing is further from the truth.

Question everything that beats common sense. When a guy is saying that all you need to do to grow three times and get into the big league is by doing this fantastic acquisition and he tells you how the combined entity can raise so much more money from the capital market, ask the fellow to show you the last company where he had a reputation for working hard or solving real problems. Stay on course. Focus on fundamentals.

Anyone who suggests that you do not need any hard foundation to quickly build a multi-storey structure or advocates overnight possibilities of great success, beware.

Another interesting thing I have observed is that while many analysts have the power of deep observation, analysis and predictive capability, there are also those who have no clue as to what they are saying. Some are just writing reports by reading other people's reports and sprinkling them with a little garnish here and there. If you are trying to learn about the future from the latter category, you have problems coming your way. The better way of knowing what is happening is to look at what is going on in the world of your customer's customer and supplier's supplier. Visit trade shows. Read three newspapers from three parts of the world. Actively watch what the best competitors are doing. Read *BusinessWeek*, *Time* and *Newsweek* on all long-haul flights. Read the *Wall Street Journal* when you can. You will have a good idea of what emergence is, where it could take you and what could leave you behind.

Finally, in order to make emergence your friend, always publish the decisional rules to the larger organization whenever you deal with a new kind of situation. Open up decisions for scrutiny and create an environment of collective learning. When you publish decisional rules and lessons learnt to the larger organization, sometimes to a small group of leaders and sometimes to people at large, you let them know what were the stakes and what the potential alternatives when you took a decision. In the process, you are upping the decisional savvy of the organization. You would be surprised how quickly these things take root and to what great advantage!

FIFTEEN

Managing Adversity

It is a beautiful Monday morning. You are getting ready to go and win the world. The phone rings. Your voice loses its pep and your expression becomes serious. Your concerned spouse is asking you, 'What's wrong?' At the other end, the caller is trying to tell you one of these:

- It is your doctor saying you have very high blood pressure
- Your best customer has just been fired and his sworn enemy has taken his place
- The venture capitalist who was to sign the deal tomorrow morning is not returning phone calls. Rumour has it that he has quit his job
- Your best buddy who had promised to join you as the head of sales and had assured you that he would bring along his no. 1 account with him has left a message that he is not joining—his family is not ready to move
- Your head of R&D has quit while the product has

just gone into beta deployment and you have no
no. 2
- Your partner wants to leave
- Your banker is refusing you the additional loan for
  expansion and you have accepted a stiff penalty
  clause for deliveries against an export order—the
  order is contingent upon that expansion plan being
  funded
- Your co-founder is going to end up in a messy
  divorce that will leave her unable to take her share
  of the load.

I could go on and on. None of the above is fictional
stuff. Among the ten people who co-founded MindTree, I
know of at least twelve major personal adversities they had
to face while coping with the task of organization building
in the first five years of the company. I am reminded of two
great authors. One is M. Scott Peck. The first sentence of his
celebrated work *The Road Less Travelled* begins like this,
'Life is difficult.' Once you accept that, everything begins to
make sense and some of it becomes bearable. The other
author who has remained in my heart is poet-novelist
Vikram Seth. As he observes, 'Long distance runners learn
to bear/Segmented pain'.

Building a great organization is about running the long
distance, and coping with different levels of physical and
mental stress. There are lots of people who can do a sprint
rather famously. Entrepreneurship, however, is not a quick
dash. When we were starting MindTree, Ashok asked me,
how long did I think it would take to build a company? I
said, five. He disagreed and told me it would be more like

ten. Six years into MindTree, I think he could not have been truer. So, it is a long haul.

I also like what Peter Drucker says. He says, you cannot solve most problems. You can only stay ahead of them. In the same vein, he says how too much of energy goes into problem-solving in organizations—many entrepreneurs who were managers in their past lives, cannot get out of the problem-solving syndrome. So what if you know how to solve problems? Could they be sucking up your energy while you should be feeding opportunity instead? Do not try to solve every problem that comes your way. See if you can change the rules of the game instead.

Webster's dictionary defines adversity as a 'condition marked by misfortune, calamity, distress, an unfortunate event or circumstance'. In other words, something patently avoidable. Yet, see what Mahatma Gandhi has to say about adversity. 'There will have to be rigid and iron discipline before we achieve anything great and enduring, and that discipline will not come by mere academic argument and appeal to reason and logic. Discipline is learnt in the school of adversity.'

Early-stage entrepreneurs are often solitary people. They keep too much to themselves and many times, it is the reason for their failure. The most important ally that you could build to cope with adversity, is a support group within the system. When senior team members can speak to each other, share their concerns, their ups and downs, they begin to pull each other up. It is like a support system akin to what you read in Lance Armstrong's book, *It's Not About the Bike: My Journey Back to Life*. In itself, the book is a great primer on overcoming adversity. In a bicycle race such as the Tour de France, teamwork is critically important. The gruelling 2200-mile race tests human endurance to the limits. Each racing team pretty much pre-decides who among its members has the best chance of winning. Thereafter, other members help him to win the race by protecting him, pushing him and helping him in every way so that he can win. That is the power of teams against adversity.

It is also important to pay attention to seemingly small issues. One of the most profound lessons is to be found in nature itself. An invisible microbe called anthrax can bring down a giant elephant. It is important to look for small signs when it comes to two things: your personal health and domestic harmony. Many entrepreneurial ventures are delivered stillborn because these two aspects were neglected. Pay serious attention to the need to stay fit—mentally and physically. Pay attention to what your spouse and children are saying. If they love what you do, you are already a winner.

The worst thing one can do is to tire out early in the game such that when adversity arrives at the front door, you challenge it with a haggard face and wobbly legs. Share the load of building the organization. Also take lots of short and certainly one annual long break—recharge yourself and build some energy for the inevitable. Create a serious passion outside of work that makes you ready for adversity when it comes.

Since adversities are inevitable and must be respected as rites of passage, the best way to handle them is to plan ahead for them. One thing that you will be happy you did is rotating key people through important functions. When different people do different things at different times, you create organizational ability to fend off the downs of life.

Three things are extremely critical when you are coping with an adversity. Be transparent, communicate well and know that more than the adversity and its outcome, you are being watched on how you are bracing the unfolding events. The way you handle any adversity remains imprinted in the minds of the people around you. The most impactful social memory is created in difficult times. The most memorable thing about mayor Rudy Giuliani of New York was his all-pervading presence during the aftermath of 9/11. The aftermath defined how the man would be remembered by posterity.

In building an enterprise, one must develop the awareness that every event is temporal. It helps to create a sense of timelessness with which we are able to journey from the source to the confluence.

COPING WITH ADVERSITY

A mail I wrote to MindTree Minds during the recession of 2002. The job of top management, in addition to dealing with adversities, is to help the organization make sense of what is going on.

My first assignment in the US was in 1990 when Wipro asked me to move to Silicon Valley to set up a beachhead. A decade later, I am back here, as co-founder of MindTree

Consulting—looking after our operations in the Americas. Until recently, I used to tell people, half in jest, that things are the same now as they were when I was in Silicon Valley. Both times, there has been a Mr Bush as President; both times, there has been recession and both times, the US has gone to war. Yet, in 1990, we had probably less than five software companies of any consequence, work was done only in client locations and the India brand did not exist. Today, we are talking about 850 or more companies directly impacted, and more than 400,000 people and their families are depending on how the world emerges from the brutal attack on the World Trade Center. Yet, there are lessons we need to pick up as we go.

1. Beyond a point, worrying does not help, you have to know as you go

Yes, the US is in a state of recession. The last one lasted three years—from 1989 to 1992. This one has been worsened by the dot.com/Internet bubble which was fanned by an overheated stock market. As a result, the crash has been louder than last time. Also, as against the last recession, today's world is so well connected, so simultaneous that if you touch something in New York, you can feel the impact in Tokyo or Bangalore the very next moment. The other aspect is how much people are exchanging information and how fast news and analysis reaches them today. This has at least one negative impact. It breeds a herd mentality at a global level. If one company in any one industry does a layoff, everyone else says, why am I not following suit? Either people say the world is going to be great place or everyone says it is coming to an end. The truth is in the median. Beyond a point no one knows the full story, no one has the full data. After all, who could predict the WTC bombing? So, we have to focus on the job at hand and move on. We have to make changes as events unfold. The important thing is in cultivating the ability to do so.

2. Companies are not slot machines

In the last few years, fund managers, venture capitalists, retail investors and a tribe of analysts had all contributed to the overheated investment climate. Unfortunately, people had lost track of a simple truth. A company is not a slot machine. But, for a moment, let us agree that it can be. The danger in that argument is that, the rules of the slot machine then apply to companies. What is the rule? A slot machine can reward only 2 per cent people only 2 per cent of the time. Change that simple rule and no one will ever set up a slot machine. We had the absolutely crazy environment in which, first of all, people regarded companies as slot machines. Worse, 98 per cent people expected to get more than they gave 98 per cent of the time. Educated people should know that that is a coveted but not feasible model. Unfortunately, in the mayhem a lot of people got greedy, set up companies with short-term gain in mind and they are falling by the wayside today. Quite sadly, they are taking a lot of people with them.

3. You do need a business plan after all

When we thought of MindTree Consulting, we began the process of thinking through the business plan fourteen months prior to launching the company. We wrote an old-fashioned business plan that ran into eighty pages. Did we have all the answers? No, we did not. Yet, we wrote the business plan—not to con someone into funding us. We believed what we wrote and used it to guide us till we rewrote the plan again. But I know of someone in the Valley who raised $100 million without having to write a business plan. Everyone got so carried away that someone said, if you have to write a business plan, you are no good. This company just wrote a sheet of Frequently Asked Questions (FAQs) and handed it to their potential investors. Two years into the game, the $100 million has evaporated and so has the company. The moral of the story is, you cannot build businesses in the air. You cannot work for people who do that. If you choose otherwise, you choose the consequences as well.

4. People need real skills to build real solutions for real customers to get real cash

People make money when real customers buy real things and pay for them. Only then, our customers can use your or my services. Those services cannot be vapourware and they cannot be devoid of the need to build solutions that 'move' things. Yet, we live in times in which these seemingly simple precepts were thrown away. Many trivialized the effort it takes, the investments you need and the time it takes before capability can be built to listen to customers, understand needs, manage them and build value for them. We also diluted the standards for hiring. We overlooked considerations and ignored simple rules of engagement. From the developer perspective, a lot of people know that they do not know. Some have no understanding of business and how things work. Armed with a rapidly acquired degree, some questionable work experience, they all flew with the H1 visa. An H1 visa takes you from place A to USA. It does not make up for, nor does it shorten, the knowledge-acquisition process and the experience building that are pre-requisites to delivering real value to paying customers.

5. Hard work and loyalty are back in fashion

In 1998, I had Gallup do a poll with 100 software engineers to accurately map the profile of the quintessential Indian software developer. Turned out, it is a 26-year-old male, decided to be a software engineer in his ninth grade, came from a nuclear family, father professional, mother homemaker, places learning, family and money as the priorities in life (in that order), is a pathological learner ('learns to learn' more than 'learns to do') and has changed 1.75 jobs in the first two years of his career. Go to anyone, anywhere in the world—they will tell you what is wrong in that model. You have to choose your career well. You have to know that you cannot be just a bundle of technical skills. There is more to life than writing code. The world needs solutions, not software, and it will take time to master that. You just cannot be tactical with your own life—sooner or later, it will all catch up. That is beginning to happen. You did not need a recession or a bin Laden to drive home that point. That is the way it works in the medical profession, in public life, in journalism, in teaching primary schoolchildren. We cannot be an exception.

6. It is going to be a long haul

How long before the current slowdown, recession, uncertain geo-political situations get better? First of all, it will get worse before it gets better. But it will get better. It is very unlikely that we will see improvements before the end of 2002. First of all, in the best case scenario, the aftermath of the WTC tragedy will take the rest of the calendar year to get sorted out. Disclaimer: Even Mr Bush does not have full knowledge and full control over what will happen, what will be the consequences and what cascading impact we will see as a result of the planned overt and covert operations. Given that fact, the investment climate will be cautious, new applications will be on hold and business justifications will be demanded before anyone spends any money. So, it will be somewhere in the middle of next year that we will come out of the penumbra of the economic effects of the next three months. And when we do come out, it will not be a start from where we left ourselves in 1999. It will be a world that will demand more personal and collective accountability. Markets, customers, investors and employers will not be the same again. Given that, you and I will need to ask ourselves some very basic questions whose answers only you and I have.

7. Skill merchants beware

In all the flux we are seeing before us, if there is one thing that is increasingly clear, it is this—people who have a purely skill view of themselves, will have more difficulty coming through. There are a lot of people out there who think that knowing Java, C++ or EJB is what it takes to assure career continuity. Unfortunately, it takes much more than that. Early in one's career, a technical person needs to learn a lot many other things. He or she needs to understand how businesses work, how to handle clients, how to work as a team and a host of other things. These can happen only one project at a time and require both patience and contemplation. Traditionally, many people have thought these are fringe issues and what really matters is the ability to churn code. Additionally, people need to learn some very non-glamorous things. The current crisis reinforces the fact that the real world depends on mainframes, legacy applications and a host of very mundane but critical things. People who have disdain for these will be in for surprises. We have to have the same attitude to the routine as we have for the latest and the best.

8. Know how much to fake

In the last two years, I am amazed as to how many people we have bred who are not themselves. Every other day, I come across people who have a disproportionate image of themselves. Worse, they believe in the self-created image. Some people look so puffed up. Strange job titles, phoney accents may look all right for a while. After some time, they can actually make a person unusable. The other day, I met an otherwise very usable middle level manager. Pre-meltdown, he got carried away and got slotted for something he did not quite fit. His company is gone but he is still perched on that imaginary place. Even making conversation is so difficult with him because he helplessly mouths jargon that makes him look like a liability. It is important to be yourself. Fancy words on a resumé do not carry one beyond a point. They actually destroy you.

9. How tactical can you, should you be?

It is important to seize the moment and take advantage of opportunities. But how far should you push the envelope? In the last few years, investors, employers, employees and customers—everyone has been guilty of developing a tactical view of the world. This was to hurt sooner or later. The current situation has hastened the process. The result is that investor money has evaporated, companies are floundering and employees are lost in a maze. In times like these, we tend to blame everything other than our own judgement. While the events around us are responsible, so are we. In Bhubaneswar, next to my in-laws' house, there used to be a private computer training institute that was always full. Whenever I visited them, my in-laws would ask me if all the boys and girls there would soon be flying off with H1 visas. I was getting tired of saying 'no'. After a while, I began to suspect my own cynicism. Today, the place is quiet as a graveyard. The question is, how could thousands of people who could not write a page of English without making a dozen mistakes and had no math skills and would not qualify a written test for a third-level engineering college, suddenly become exportable computer wizards? Did they themselves not know this? Did their parents not realize the improbability of it all? We can blame the slowdown. On the other hand, we are the slowdown.

10. The world will move on. Will you be there?

The Federal Reserve Bank chairman Alan Greenspan says that the only thing certain about a recession is that it gets over. I could say the same thing about war and associated crises that we are going to witness. That is how the world has always worked. Our parents and their parents have seen larger crises. It so happens that our share of growing up is coming to us after a protracted period of what looks like good times. Having said that, things will come full circle. As that happens, some will survive and some will be hurt. Rather than worry about either, it is a good time to do some deep reflection and come to terms with realism. It is also a good time to take a larger, more comprehensive view of one's career and make some solid investments towards that. It is also a time to rethink one's perception of some old-fashioned things like focus on fundamentals, hard work, loyalty and building real value for real customers. Are you ready?

SIXTEEN

From Idea to IPO

Quite honestly, I did not want to include this chapter as part of this book. The reason being it is a distracting subject for someone who is yet to start a venture. The allure, the glitter of an IPO—initial public offering—can be so overpowering that you may neglect the basics. It is the dream of many entrepreneurs to raise a company that is seen as worthy of being taken public, with thousands coming forward to oversubscribe its initial public offering. In the process, they can get to offload some of their stocks and make a huge amount of money. Unfortunately, many people do not realize that the event of going public is not a teenage party. The primary objective for taking your company public cannot be to offload your shares or to make a killing for yourself.

The primary objective of doing an IPO is to raise additional money from the investing public so that you further expand the business and build even greater value for your future investors. That value must help the investor get a return higher than what his bank deposit earns.

There are several considerations one must have before thinking of an IPO. A predictable revenue stream, the organization's depth and maturity, clarity on future plans, a strategy for top management succession and, of course, timing.

There is also a certain cost to doing an IPO. When you take your company through the process, it requires preparation for months. You appoint a merchant banker, you go to multiple cities and brief the investing public, you set up hugely expensive mechanisms for reporting, audit and accountability. Given all these, doing an IPO for anything less than a large amount of money makes no sense. What is 'large' is situational. But know that unless there is need for a substantially large amount of money—forty or fifty million dollars for a listing in smaller exchanges to at least a hundred million in international exchanges—it is simply a wasteful exercise. For smaller sums, you could easily look at private equity funding.

If you are about to take your company public, you need to be clear about how you would create value by using the money you are going to raise. That cash comes interest-free, unlike a bank loan. You need to pay the investor a return on that investment. You may or may not give out dividends against it, depending on how the business fares from time to time. To most investors, however, dividend is less important. What is more important is significant capital appreciation in a relatively short time. That means, you have to have the ability to build a valuable company on a sustained basis. When you have the plan clear and the maturity to execute that plan, you take the company public as a vehicle for raising large amounts of interest-free cash. It is also a time for some of your venture capitalists to offload a part of their holding.

In short, taking your company to the IPO event brings with itself huge responsibilities and accountability. It is better not to think about it right in the beginning, and focus on the organization-building process instead.

While timing is critical, many people would suggest that you should experience eight sequential months of steady growth before you think of going public.

When you make an IPO, you agree to subject the organization to close scrutiny—day in and day out. By the press, by the analyst community, shareholders, regulators and the government itself. In recent times, there has been a huge amount of outcry against organizations that have defrauded their shareholders. Consequently, in many countries, there is insistence on setting up special regulatory and compliance mechanisms which in themselves can involve a huge annual investment. In the US, the cost of compliance for a new entity going public is estimated at an annual $4 to 5 million.

So, unless you need the additional cash, remain a sub-IPO company for as long as you can. It gives you so much more freedom to manage and navigate the company without all the glare and accountability that the 'quarterly results' treadmill brings along.

Though you may not want to take the company to an IPO event for as long as you can, it is still a great idea to pretend that you are public after a year or two of operations. It is the best way to bring in professionalism, create a culture of accountability and make governance understood across the rank and file. And it makes people deliver on their forecasts of revenues and profits.

The thing the stock market hates most is unpredictable and uncertain revenues and profitability that yo-yoes. It is often said that traders prefer bad news to uncertainty. Because, once they know that something bad has happened, they know how to deal with it. But they cannot handle unpredictable performance. They swiftly punish such stocks. Consequently, a public company must have great control over its destiny so that despite a number of market variables, it can deliver growth and profitability quarter after quarter. Without that confidence, markets can be extremely punishing and all the good work done by the founding team can get washed away.

Sometimes, it is better to sell off your company than to do an IPO—especially when you do not have the confidence to embrace the huge additional load that comes with it.

When an organization is mature enough, has visibility over its future and knows how to deliver predictably and needs serious cash to expand, it is time to mull over the IPO process. This must begin a year before the event. The choice of the merchant banker is the most crucial to be taken at that point. In addition to that, it is very important to train the entire management team in the disciplines required as well as to provide them with the knowledge of regulatory compliances. These include externally focused legal compliances as well as internally focused ones that deal with insider trading and other such issues.

Taking your company public involves dilution of

ownership. Attention must be paid to how much dilution should be made in what progression—sometimes companies create a financial vision for five years after the IPO for successive fund raising. They may follow a domestic IPO with an international listing like an issue of American Depository Receipts (ADR) and so on. Today, most countries allow multiple listing—so it becomes important that one has a clear idea about why the company is listing in whichever exchange and in what sequence it would raise more capital.

One of the greatest advantages of taking a company public is the brand awareness it creates. If the company does well, it remains high in the minds of investors, the media, the analyst community, and all these create a favourable buzz for new customers who may look for stability and brand recall. Conversely, if a publicly traded company destroys investor wealth, it can adversely impact customer and employee perception—particularly in the initial periods.

In many countries, taking a company public and thereafter growing it is considered to be better handled by 'professional management'. Thus, sometimes the founders bow out and the company brings in so-called professional managers who then run the company. This is not necessarily the case with every company, nor is it necessarily the recommended approach. There are enough instances to the contrary: Apple Computer, for instance, where after a John Scully had moved out, a Steve Jobs was brought back to save the company from disaster. Companies like Intel and Microsoft and Infosys have kept growing with the original set of founders and gone on to build huge investor wealth decade after decade.

In all this, two things largely determine the issue. How much energy is the original team still left with? Secondly, does it have what it takes to run with the newer sets of challenges of growth, complexity and accountability that come with the option of IPO. I give below Rostow Ravanan's advice on taking the company public.

ASSESSING WHETHER YOUR COMPANY IS READY TO GO PUBLIC: ROSTOW RAVANAN'S WORDS OF ADVICE

Business-related issues:

- The rule of the public market is that the company gets evaluated on three variables—growth, predictability and profitability. The company needs to score at the median level on two parameters and very high on at least one. For example, you should grow at least three times the rate of growth of the market leader if you are less than half its profitability, assuming you have reasonable visibility on revenues for four quarters. Markets understand that no company scores 10 on 10 on all three parameters. What the company needs to do is to plot where it is and how the trade-off between these parameters will happen as it goes forward.
- Risk to revenues, that is, customer concentration, dependency on a few markets/services/products etc. Are you exposed to external risks, e.g. currency/interest rate movements, access to a particular resource (e.g. a mine) or governmental controls.
- Scalability of the business—will the business be able to

grow faster if you had more capital, does the company know what it takes to scale the business?

- Comparisons—are you 'one-of-a-kind' or are there comparables in the market. Normally, it is more difficult to take a unique company to market, because it would be more difficult to explain the business to investors.
- Has the business matured? If your business needs more time on the runway to achieve critical mass and reach escape velocity, it is not a good IPO candidate. A public company comes under the harsh spotlight of investor scrutiny each quarter. The stock market is a fickle admirer. If you deliver as promised, you will have glory heaped on you. If you miss your numbers for two quarters in succession you will see your stock price hammered. If your business is not at a stage where you can manage it on a quarterly cycle, and needs a long-term view, don't raise money from the public.

Operations/process/financial/legal issues:

- Is your profitability comparable to the industry leaders? If not, do you have a clear roadmap on how to get there?
- Are you able to close your books by the first week of the month with >95 per cent accuracy? Are you able to sustain this month after month?
- Review all your customer contracts—what is the revenue potential and duration of the contracts? Usually, the longer term contracts you have, the better the perception of the investors.
- Do you have adequate insurance to cover professional liability, IPO-related financial statements etc.

- Who are your auditors? If you are working with a small firm, but their partner is related to one of your founders, now is the time to change to a more credible one.
- Do you have any pending disputes, with a customer, government agency, past employee or a supplier? The cleaner the legal slate, the better it is.
- Who are your legal advisers? Again, it is important to get leading advisers who will be able to add value, and have multi-disciplinary service capability. You need to be comfortable that you are within the boundaries of the law, under all statutes applicable to you, e.g. foreign exchange, labour, tax, corporate, environment protection.
- Do you have the bandwidth to manage the quarterly pressure to report results, hold analyst calls, explain the business to investors, meet investors periodically, answer probing questions, do roadshows?

People-related issues:

- How strong is your next tier leadership team? Do you have savvy, articulate people who are at ease facing savvy investors?
- Do you have a second and third tier leadership team—both to project to the market as an indication of your scalability and longevity, as well as to take up the workload from the primary team, because they will be distracted from running the actual business. This applies to all functions in the organization.
- What is the composition of your board? Statutorily, you need 50 per cent of the board to be independent

if you have an executive chairman and one-third of the board to be independent if you have a non-executive chairman. VC/Private equity investors, customers, vendors and others who have a material/financial relationship with the company, as well as relatives of key executives are not considered independent.

- What kind of stock option plans do you have, are they compliant with the applicable regulations in the venue where you are proposing to list.

- Will you lose people after the IPO? You may have people who are staying with the company only for the sake of the financial returns and with the financial upside they will get after the IPO, many may be tempted to leave.

- Do you have a good Investor Relations team? Your Investor Relations team needs to be thoroughly aware of your business, its drivers and dynamics and the competition, and be savvy in handling investors, financial analysts and the media. It will be disastrous if you don't have a good Investor Relations team, because the load will then fall on the CEO, CFO and other business heads, plus investors will form a poor opinion of the company in their interactions with the Investor Relations team. This is as much about marketing and communication as it is about the financial stuff. Each such interaction is a touch point to the external world and has business benefits.

- Do your people have a long-term orientation to grow the business, manage the business sensibly, and not succumb to taking short cuts to meet quarterly numbers? The temptation to stay on top of the quarters' numbers has been the ruin of many good companies.

Where do you want to list?

The decision on the listing venue needs to be taken with many criteria in mind. Some of the important criteria are:

- Where are you headquartered? The legal requirements of countries differ on accessing domestic and international capital markets. This needs to be studied in depth and understood thoroughly. It is not advisable to tamper with your corporate structure; e.g. move your holding company to a tax haven like Mauritius, or to list in an international stock exchange without going into the proposition in depth. As in all other aspects of your business, taking decisions with short-term gains in mind will bring complications in the long run.
- The IPO is a platform to raise capital as well as increase visibility for your company. So, you should study where your customers are located. Does it make sense to list in that geography so that awareness of your brand increases?
- Valuation: given that you are issuing shares and raising money, where will you get the highest valuation?
- Taxation: many countries have different tax consequences on capital gains, dividend income etc. This is an important aspect because one venue could give you higher valuation, but another could give you better tax rates, so that your effective realization could be higher in the latter venue.
- Costs: it is very important to keep costs in mind and

not be overly swayed by valuations. Ultimately, all the costs of the business have to be picked up by either investors or customers. So, don't lose sight of the costs. While analysing the costs, you need to keep in mind both the cost of the IPO itself (e.g. underwriting and legal fees, printing, distribution, roadshows, travel, listing fees) and ongoing costs (roadshows, travel, investor relations, cost of compliance, risks, insurance).

SEVENTEEN

Reasons Start-ups Fail

Most start-ups that fail, do so in the very first year of being born. There are several reasons. Usually, however, the commonest reason is differences among founders. I want you to know two things in this regard. One, friendship and a business partnership are not the same thing. Sometimes, friendship clouds the objectivity that business partnership requires. A good way to figure out whether your friend will make a good business partner is to ask the fundamental question—what is the value your friend (or relative) brings to the business? If the answer is a large affirmative, you will find ways and means of dealing with the inter-personal issues that are bound to crop up in the transition from being close friends to successful business partners.

The second thing you should know is that irrespective of your emotional closeness, in building your business, differences will crop up. At the first sign of differences, do not panic. If people work with each other, they must encourage healthy debate and some serious differences—

otherwise the business will not do well.

All direction setting, formulation of policy and issue resolution must be preceded by bringing forth alternative views. I know of situations where friend-turned-entrepreneurs take differences personally and interpret the alternative point of view as a sign of disloyal behavior.

Relationship cracks among founders also appear because of unresolved role clarity and ownership pattern. Because of closeness, people find it awkward to settle issues like who would own how much, who would be the no. 1 and who no. 2. They create ambiguities to skirt these issues and inevitably one day, things become intolerable and cracks show up. By then, it is too late to sort things out. However delicate the issues may seem, address them upfront.

I think that the second reason start-ups fail is because they are underfunded. One must be very realistic about two things. How much money will it take to build the business? Secondly, when should you raise money and from whom?

My first entrepreneurial experience was at the age of 28. It lasted all of three years before going belly up. I had joined two senior industry colleagues, who had brought in their paltry savings. I had no money to invest and I was allowed to subscribe to the equity from my payroll. Between ourselves, we created the company and grew it to a three-centre, twenty-people company. The company was in the corporate training business. It had no external funding. In India of 1985, banks did not lend money to such organizations. The concept of venture capital did not exist. So, we had to meet the capital and revenue expenses of the company from the cash flow of the business. Hardly the way to go. Thus, even though the company had good clients, good margins and high utilization, it was a hand-to-mouth existence. This may still work when one is not seeking volume growth and expansion.

Very soon, poor funding led to inter-personal issues and the company folded up. The other thing about funding is that one must have a three-to-five-year roadmap on how much money will be needed, in what tranches, and how the money would be raised and utilized. Not only should one have a clear view of that, as I have said before, it is important to raise money well before you run out of cash. Always raise funds when you still have six months to a year of working capital in the bank. Otherwise, people will take advantage of your situation.

Start-ups fail because they succumb to what I call the 'deadly embrace' syndrome. It happens most often through two mistakes. Getting excited about a point technology (as against a family of product or technology ideas with a roadmap) or getting locked into a single customer relationship that is born out of patronage.

Consider this: two techies come together to start a company. A friend in the US agrees to give business in return of ownership. Before they know it, they have a few hundred people working on the customer's project. This creates a warm, cocoon-type of relationship. The two friends find this a great way to show early success, but that success also traps them. They do not pound the streets for work from elsewhere. Soon there is a downturn in the customer's business. He asks for substantial rate reduction, then begins to default on payments. Other complications follow.

From the beginning, de-risk three things: technology overdependence, customer overdependence and geography overdependence. At a senior management level, it is important to make the right investments, fan out and make sure you reach a progressive state in the first three years by which no single customer has greater than 10 per cent of your business share. In five years, if you can reduce your geographic spread such that no one geography contributes to more than 50 to 60 per cent of your business, you should congratulate yourself for a good job done.

The next reason start-ups fail is because the founders do not let go. It is that big tussle between ownership and growth, between perfection-seeking and expanding through delegation. We need to spend some time in analysing both these situations.

But before we do that, it is very important to answer one basic question. What is the personal vision one has for starting the company? Do I want to be a shopkeeper or do I want to create an institution that will survive me? There is absolutely no harm in settling for one over the other. But one must be truthful to oneself and the people around and answer the question in earnest.

A shopkeeper builds value through tight control over everything and must have complete ownership. Lesser the delegation, higher the personal comfort. Direct oversight helps the shopkeeper deliver value to an intimate set of customers. On the other hand, if the same person wants to create a chain of shops or a franchisee network, it becomes a different ball game. In the latter, one has to delegate, one has to let go. The important issue is to determine for oneself, what is my long-term goal (read five years) and which of the two choices is true to my personal style. It is the clash between ambition and the personal style of owners that causes the undoing of many an enterprise.

Start-ups fail because of poor governance. Many people confuse the difference between what is owned by the business versus what is owned by the founder. V.G. Siddhartha is India's largest exporter of coffee and he owns the very successful Café Coffee Day chain. Once, Siddhartha and his wife took my family out for dinner. My daughters Neha and Niti wanted to drink coffee after dinner and Siddhartha took us all to one of his cafes. After we all had our lattes, a waiter promptly brought him the bill and he paid the cash. Very few entrepreneurs would do that. Not only would they walk out without paying in their own establishments, their spouses and children would do the same.

That brings me to the second part of governance—it is about accountability. The owner of a business is first and foremost accountable to the business—irrespective of the size of the ownership, a questioning board or any other external factor. If the owner does not hold himself accountable for every expense and every decision, the business gets mired by the limiting behaviour of the owner. It can never outgrow that.

Lastly, governance is about resisting the temptation of bringing in kith and kin. The moment you get comfort in the relationship blood builds, you make your business serve that relationship ahead of other considerations. Having your kith and kin as decision makers, employees and suppliers, per se, is not a wrong thing to do. But most certainly, they come in the way if an organization has larger ambitions.

Start-ups fail because the owners get carried away with their new-found status. In Cisco, the 35,000-people strong networking giant (2005 revenue: $28.8 billion), I am told, there used to be an adage: 'Do not believe your own press.' The day you start believing your own press, you begin to fall in love with your image and start drifting away from reality. You love your image so much that it blurs the image in the rear-view mirror.

Entrepreneurs are usually ego-driven type 'A' people who rally the troops, build collective ambition and push forward. A little bit of embellishment is like their vitamin supplement. But if that becomes their staple food, there is a problem in store.

Many times, a start-up fails because it tries to be too big, too soon and in the process, does things which are not its core competence. This is a tough one. On the one hand, you are told not to be overdependent on any one technology, customer or geography and to take risks and innovate, and on the other you are told not to venture into things you do not understand. It is indeed a difficult path to tread, balancing risk and reward. Yet, a few things are important.

When you do get into a new area, go whole hog. One of the senior members of the team must take personal responsibility to make it work—do not trivialize any business. In addition, do not get carried away by the 'merger and acquisition' mania before the organization has been able to fully stand on its two legs. Historically, 90 per cent of the mergers and acquisitions do not work and invariably they destroy the pre-merger value of both entities. It is a serious distraction for top management and must not be pursued too soon in the life of a company.

Start-ups fail because of a wrong choice of investors and the consequential mismatch in expectations. The downstream impacts are so colourful that one could write a novel on them. So, we will just stop at that.

Start-ups fail because the founding team is more in love with the idea of getting rich than with the concept of building value. I meet numerous people who are bitten by the famous Silicon Valley mindset of building a company, just so that it could be acquired as soon as possible. If that is the sole reason, it is your people who would be the first to know what's on your mind and that would dictate their level of true involvement. Whether you get acquired or go public is a secondary and an eventual issue. What must engage your mind is building real products or services and getting paying customers for them.

Start-ups fail also because of health and family reasons. The journey of the entrepreneur is mentally and physically taxing. When you build a company on your own and devote five years to it, the energy burn is equivalent to twice what it would be if you were a typical salaried executive in a large company. However intense your corporate job may be, however much of an 'intrapreneur' someone may be, it is never the same. In building your own company, when you do experience a high or a low, much of the time, you are alone. It is therefore absolutely important that you do six things seriously.

- Workout thrice a week. Learn to meditate.
- Enlist the support of your spouse and children.

- Do something other than work. Spend time outdoors if you can.
- Take many small breaks and one large break every year.
- Do not neglect the smallest sign of a medical ailment.
- Be comfortable with yourself.

EIGHTEEN

Lessons in Entrepreneurship from the Indian IT Industry

In closing, I want to talk to you about a few lessons from the Indian IT industry which has opted to walk a different path—very different from the ones many other traditional Indian businesses have trodden. As a result, the Indian IT industry has been able to lead India to her rightful place in the world, in this area at least.

There was a time when an Indian arriving at any international airport was deemed to be an illegal immigrant or a taxi driver. Today, even if this is so, people assume that since he is Indian, he probably writes software code!

In my opinion, where you reach is a function of your vision and more than that, it is a function of the values you choose for yourself. The IT industry could become truly global because of several conscious choices it made, breaking away from a developing country mindset. Let us take a moment and glean a few lessons from the industry without godfathers so that we can create many memorable enterprises in every other field that will grow to serve the world, build unusual new *value* and create *legacy*. Because, in my mind, these three words best exemplify what entrepreneurship is all about: developing a service-centric mindset, the creation of unusual value and finally, a deep sense of leaving something behind. Without these, you do not become an entrepreneur worth the mention.

LESSON # 1. TO BE WORLD-CLASS, YOU BEGIN AND END WITH QUALITY

The first lesson from the IT industry is about its adherence to Quality. Quality begins only when we admit that we are here to serve. Entrepreneurs who want to build great organizations must deeply believe in the basic tenet that they are there to 'serve' others. Most acts of entrepreneurship are motivated by someone's ego, the desire to be rich and powerful. These are legitimate reasons. Yet, they are not enough to create memorable companies. The only way to build great institutions is to remain focused on the simple aim of creating great quality, at affordable cost and having the product or service delivered the way the customer loves it. The unstated rule of this game is that we have to keep improving quality while constantly lowering the cost and improving the way we deliver. That was how Japan won the automobile race. That is how we have, so far, won the software race. More than half of the world's SEI CMMi level 5 companies—that denotes the highest level at which someone's process maturity can be assessed at—are in India. The IT industry embraced the quality mantra way back in the 1990s, when the world was still questioning the relevance of quality in the software world. Rather than join the controversy, we joined the cause. It was a repeat of what the Japanese had done in the 1960s. While principles of quality were developed in the US through the 1940s and the 1950s, there were few takers of what proponents of total quality— people like Deming and Juran—had evangelized. A war-ravaged Japan embraced every word they spoke and redefined what the term 'Made in Japan' conveyed. To build a great enterprise, we have to breathe, dream and deliver quality— ahead of what the customer is asking for and ahead of what the competition is doing.

LESSON # 2. IT IS ABOUT WHAT YOU KNOW, NOT WHO YOU KNOW

The second lesson we all must take away from the IT industry is something very profound. This industry runs on the principle of 'what' you know, not 'who' you know. There is a world of difference between the two starting points.

In India, thanks to our feudal history, followed by a few hundred years of foreign rule, two interesting aspects of the business persona evolved. First, the fact that kings ruled us for thousands of years, created a mindset of largesse in business people. It continues even today—people align themselves to political power centres to get a contract, get access to capital or corner other benefits. When that becomes your core competence, learning the language of world-class business becomes your core incompetence. If the primary focus of management is to observe, align with and live off power centres, they cannot generate power by themselves.

The second deeply ingrained cultural issue with Indian businessmen is the drug of intermediation. Because we were ruled for many hundred years by people of foreign origin—people whose language we did not understand—a whole breed of Indians came up whose job was to become 'intermediaries'. Sometimes, knowing an intermediary became more important than knowing the rulers. Rulers changed, the intermediaries remained. The licence raj gave fresh impetus to this culture. Over time, this has become a deep-seated addiction. Once you build your business on the strength of who you know, and not what you know, you will be on that treadmill. Over the years, the speed at which you work the treadmill will only increase.

The IT industry is a notable exception to this rule. It is amazing how the successful IT companies have seldom done business through intermediaries and commission agents. When you build your own business, make sure you deal with the customer directly as much as possible.

LESSON # 3. GREAT ORGANIZATIONS ARE BUILT BY PEOPLE WITH AN 'ABUNDANCE' MINDSET

The third lesson to be learnt from the IT industry is a mindset of abundance and not scarcity. When you build an abundance mindset, you are buoyed by it. In 1993, I was one among many people who were invited to the inauguration of the Infosys campus. On that occasion, the chairman, N.R. Narayana Murthy, made a public vow that Infosys would strive to make a hundred Infoscions (not employees) millionaires by the year 2000! It was unheard of that an entrepreneur would evaluate his success or the success of the enterprise based on how much wealth it could create for people who work for the organization! As a result, Infosys has become a global company, buoyed by the spirit of shared wealth creation. The wealth created by an enterprise is not private property just because its seed was in the capital of the entrepreneur. At MindTree, we began by stating that every MindTree Mind would be a part-owner of the company. It is not a symbolic statement—it is a firm departure from an outdated, feudal mindset. That mindset prevents companies from becoming globally admired and sustainable.

LESSON # 4. A GREAT ENTERPRISE IS BUILT BY PEOPLE WHO ARE PROUD TO PAY THEIR TAXES RIGHT

The fourth lesson from the IT industry is in its pride in paying taxes right. You will never hear about Narayana Murthy, Azim Premji or Ashok Soota losing sleep over the sound of the taxman's footsteps. These people, like all of us in the industry, are proud to pay their taxes right. In the last many years that I can recall, every single year, I have received a tax refund by mail from the Income Tax Office of Salary Ward, Bangalore, without ever visiting them or being visited by them. That simple thing is not understood by most Indian businesses. We overplay the issue of complex government regulations and corruption to justify our personal tax evasion. The primary qualification for a would-be businessman becomes the ability to fudge accounts and evade taxes—as if that is all there is to creating a great enterprise. Great nations and great economies are built when people pay their taxes right.

I am not blind to the fact that sometimes we all suffer because of a poorly drafted law or a poor interpretation of it. At MindTree, when we are faced with something like that, we first pay the tax and then we fight it out. We do not smear our face because someone else is in the wrong.

LESSON # 5. TO BE WORLD-CLASS, YOU HAVE TO BE HIERARCHY-FREE

The fifth lesson from the IT industry is its total disregard for hierarchy. At MindTree, our car parks have reserved slots for only two kinds of people—customers and people with disabilities. If Ashok Soota comes late to work, his car gets the farthest slot from the portico. We do not have special toilets for 'owners', we eat in the same cafeteria with everyone else and all the rules that apply to every other person in the organization, apply to us first. In Wipro, the joy (and the nightmare) for a travelling sales person was discovering Azim Premji as one's neighbour in the spartan guest houses the company maintained. Any person, irrespective of his or her level in the organization, can send a mail to a Narayana Murthy or an Ashok Soota, openly questioning company policy, direction or practices, and these people admit that they are accountable. When they do that, they lay down the importance of transparency and governance—two critical requirements to become a global player in any business. It is amazing how social memory gets created when leaders set the example.

I must share with you this small but significant anecdote that exemplifies the concept of hierarchy in most businesses.

A few years ago, the wife of an industrialist was showing me around their workplace. A part we were about to enter had been cordoned off for some genuine reason. As we were walking up the staircase to that area, a security guard stopped us. This vastly embarrassed and enraged the lady. She briskly ignored him, entered the area and pulled up someone senior as to how the security guard was indiscriminate and ill-informed. Read, how come he did not recognize her? That night, I could well imagine the dressing down the security guard received. Rest assured, he in his entire life, will never question any pretty woman who speaks English with a hint of arrogance. In the IT industry, that man would have been fêted, his photo would have been on the intranet and he would have received a spot award. At MindTree, security personnel are under strict instruction not to salute any of us. Their job is to be vigilant, not respectful.

LESSON # 6. LEADERS EXEMPLIFY PERSONAL INTEGRITY

The sixth lesson from the IT industry is about the unimpeachable personal integrity of the people at the helm of affairs. When I was in Wipro, Premji had invited Narayana Murthy to speak to the Corporate Executive Council. Narayana Murthy was speaking about the personal standards of integrity followed at Infosys. Even at that time, when corporate governance was not a buzzword, his wife had to pay for her own expenses while travelling with Narayana Murthy.

There are times when I travel on business with my wife, Susmita, accompanying me. If she and I share a meal at a hotel by ourselves, I make it a point to write on the restaurant bill that half of it should be debited to her. It is quite another story that she pays under protest. According to her, while she eats 25 per cent of the food, she has to pay for 50 per cent of the bill! Companies like MindTree, Wipro and Infosys live by the principles of complete transparency and integrity down the organization. These are articulated and evangelized by the top management. When there is the inevitable, occasional breach, irrespective of the quantum of offence, who is involved and what is at stake, the organization deals with the matter with immediacy and seriousness.

LESSON # 7. GREAT ENTERPRISES BELIEVE IN SETTING UP HAIRY, AUDACIOUS GOALS

The seventh lesson to be gleaned from the IT industry is about the linkage between great success and setting up of hairy, audacious goals. The linkage between greatness and size of the vision was officially discussed at the World Economic Forum a few years ago when a study presented showed that the one thing common among all noteworthy organizations in the world is the size of the goal they always set for themselves. They never, ever made their dreams hostage to the constraints of their times. They never thought of the future as something connected to the present by an incremental staircase. To them, the future was irrationally large, unbelievably beautiful and they coveted it so much, they made it happen. When I was sent to the Silicon Valley in 1990 to set up shop for Wipro, the Reserve Bank of India did not permit us to buy foreign exchange to open an office. Those were the days when you had to get permission to buy the dollars needed for expenses overseas. So, Wipro's office was my two-bedroom apartment in Cupertino. I bought an electronic typewriter and a fax machine for a couple of hundred dollars and declared myself open. Little could anyone imagine that the same organization would become a multi-billion-dollar, household word in the global IT industry in fifteen years from then! Wipro always set up for itself monstrous goals and created the path towards them. Infosys is a great example of setting up many such goals too— whether it is the goal to produce the first hundred millionaires in the IT industry, or to become the first Indian company to be listed on NASDAQ.

LESSON # 8. WORLD-CLASS ORGANIZATIONS ARE DEEPLY INCLUSIVE

No vision in human history has ever been delivered without creating inclusion. The one significant difference between the IT industry and all others is the amount of substantive and not symbolic inclusion it has created. Inclusion is not about building temples and charities and at the same time, maintaining a safe distance between the entrepreneur and the smallest person who works for the organization. I want to explain the concept of inclusion to you at three levels— at the level of information sharing , at the level of caring for those who are close to you and finally at the level of those who are only remotely connected to you.

First, let us talk about inclusion by 'information sharing'. Information is everything. If information is not shared or shared selectively, we can never build inclusion. If we cannot trust our own people, how can our customers trust them?

Now, let me tell you about caring for people who are close to you. I want to tell you about a man called

V. Chandrasekaran—who is the chief executive officer of Aztec. Known popularly as VC to colleagues in the industry, he is an example of building inclusion by deeply caring for people close to him. One such man for whom VC has deep caring is Inder. After dropping out of Class 7th in a small hamlet named Guru in Ratu Thana near Ranchi, Inder ran away to Delhi where life brought him and VC together. After that, over the decades, VC has moved places in life while Inder has taken charge of his mobility as driver and man Friday. VC has remained as loyal to Inder as Inder has been to VC. When Inder chose his wife, VC and his wife got them married, and when VC built his own house in Bangalore, at the same time, he also bought Inder an apartment, so that he too has a respectable, secure and comfortable living. But more importantly, VC and his wife took personal interest in his son Suryadev's education— they enrolled him at the best school in the neighborhood. Today, a young, self-assured Suryadev is at the top of his class and has dreams to be a space scientist!

VC's personal success is not about how he has raised his own two children—his success is in irreversibly changing the track for Inder. Very recently, when VC's son got married and friends from the IT industry were invited to a five-star hotel for the reception, guess who were receiving guests and mingling with everyone? Inder and Suryadev.

Now let me explain the concept of inclusion that involves people whom we would never meet, people who are often twice or thrice removed from our zone of interaction. When Infosys was to be listed on NASDAQ, the entire NASDAQ team firmly believed that the floor price could do well with an increase by another quarter of a cent. When they insisted that Infosys should up the price, chairman Narayana Murthy turned down the suggestion. He said, if that was so, let the investors see that immediate gain for themselves and feel good about their investment—rather than Infosys pocket the increase. Multiplied a million times over, that quarter would have been big enough money for anyone else in Narayana Murthy's shoes!

To him, however, the collective goodwill of people he would never see meant much more than the guaranteed prospect of an immediate gain.

The IT industry has come up to be what it is today, because in every deal, it leaves something behind on the table so that people come back to deal again.

LESSON # 9. THE ORGANIZATION'S RESOURCES ARE NOT 'MY' RESOURCES

The ninth lesson from the IT industry is about making a clear distinction between personal resources and organizational resources. Just because you start a company does not mean you 'own' it. My company's resources are not *my* resources. The truth is that such misuse of organizational resources is quite commonplace among business owners and industrialists in India. You will seldom see such impoverishment of the mind in the IT industry.

LESSON # 10. ADMIRABLE ORGANIZATIONAL PROSPERITY BEGINS WITH AUSTERE LEADERSHIP

The tenth lesson from the IT industry is about austerity. If you are waiting at the venue of a conference in Bangalore, what car do you think you are most likely to spot Nandan

Nilekani, CEO of Infosys, in? A Toyota Qualis. Most people think, if you have it, you must flaunt it. That may well be the way many lead their lives; leaders in the IT industry stand out with their sense of connectedness with the larger reality. Greater wealth comes to those who respect its power to create change and look at themselves as a mere conduit. An entrepreneur is like a municipal water pipeline, which is meant to convey the water, not quench its own thirst.

LESSON # 11. IT IS ABOUT ORDINARY PEOPLE DELIVERING EXTRA-ORDINARY RESULTS

The eleventh lesson from the IT industry is about its ability to deliver extraordinary results with ordinary people. My father was an honest government servant with a last salary drawn of Rs. 300 in 1967. Co-founder Janakiraman's father was a village postmaster in Tamil Nadu. The father of another co-founder, Parthasarathy, was a travelling ticket collector in the Indian Railways and Ashok Soota's father was a colonel in the Army. The father of yet another founder, Kalyan, was a geologist in the coalmines and that of the youngest founder, Rostow, was an accountant.

That tradition is pervasive in the IT industry. Recently, I was looking at the demographic profile of 300 young engineers who had just joined MindTree from premium engineering colleges around the country. Each one had come to MindTree, not on the strength of whom she knew, but solely on the basis of what she knew. Far from being privileged, one in three came from a rural, agricultural background. One in five was from a small business owner's household. The rest were from families of salaried folks of the neighborhood. How affluent are these families? One in three has a combined household income of less than Rs. 10,000 per month. The median household income is a modest Rs. 16,000!

You know what is interesting about us? When the time comes—one of these people will become the chairman of MindTree. By design, that position will not be open to the children of the founders.

LESSON # 12. PLAY IT BY THE BOOK

The twelfth and the final lesson from the IT industry is that you can become world-class by playing it by the book. The IT industry was not created by people born with a silver spoon. The dice was loaded against them as much as it was loaded against anyone else. The mediocrity of the system was not their excuse to take short cuts in life. They were clear in their minds that it takes time to build sustainable enterprise. Each leader is deeply driven by the desire to be admired, ahead of the need to be successful in the ordinary sense of the term.

Here is an industry that has delivered two things worth noticing. One, it has made India a brand. Two, it has delivered the brand without bending the rules. It has proven that such things may take time, they may call for greater resolution, but they can be done. Even out of India!

Thus, the Indian IT industry is just a proof of concept— in the years ahead, it must be outdone in size and importance by many other enterprises, in many other fields. By playing it by the book.

Some day, when you build your own enterprise, treat it

the way a small farmer treats his land. Some years, the harvest is good. There are also years when a hailstorm comes from nowhere and razes the standing crop that is ready to go home. Some years, he just looks at the sky as the clouds pass by without stopping. Yet, he does not give up. Uncomplainingly, he gets up again. Once more, goes back to till his land.

Great value is born out of the feeling that an enterprise is like a piece of land we all have been given. Our charter is to create unusual, lasting value out of it—value that nourishes other lives. Value that builds greater value. In building it, sustainability and not chimera must guide entrepreneurial vision.

The Last Word

You did not read a 'how to' book before you fell in love. Yet, in some ways, the books on romance may have helped.

You really do not need to read this book—for that matter *any book*—to start your own enterprise.

And lest I forget, no amount of reading about romance is equal to the act of falling in love. Like the many books on romance, I hope this one will only help you in some small way every now and then. But remember, the actual experience is in the enactment.

So, go on and do it.

Additional Resources

Books you should read

On entrepreneurship, business basics and corporate governance:

1. Hirsch, Robert D. and Peters, Michael P. *Entrepreneurship.* New York: McGraw-Hill Irwin, 2002.
2. McCormack, Mark H. *What They Don't Teach You at Harvard Business School: Notes From a Street-Smart Executive.* Toronto: Bantam Books, 1986.
3. *All About Integrity*—available on request at www.mindtree.com

On coping with adversity:

4. Armstrong, Lance. *It's Not About the Bike: My Journey Back to Life.* New York: Berkley Books, 2001.
5. Morrell, Margot and Capparell, Stephanie. *Shackleton's Way: Leadership Lessons from the Great Antarctic Explorer.* London: Nicholas Brealey, 2002.

On sales and marketing:

6. Kotler, Philip, *Principles of Marketing*, New Jersey: Prentice-Hall, 1983.
7. Ries, Al and Trout, Jack. *Positioning: The Battle for Your Mind.* New York: McGraw-Hill, 1981.

On vision and other things:

8. Bach, Richard. *Jonathan Livingstone Seagull*. London: Pan Books, 1973.
9. Coelho, Paulo. *The Alchemist*. London: HarperCollins, 1988.

On building a realistic assessment of your self:

10. Your last three appraisals. Read the improvement areas shown by your bosses and talk to your spouse or your best friend about them, focus on the areas of improvement and dig deeper into them. See if they impair your ability to be an entrepreneur.
11. Peer appraisals. If you have a formal 360-degree appraisal system in your current organization and have the feedback for the last three consecutive years, read up what your peers said about you and see what was common as feedback in all three years. Peers usually are your harshest critics and through them you can find out the real you.

Entrepreneurship Resources

1. The Indus Entrepreneur—www.tie.org
2. The Wadhwani Foundation—www.wadhwani-foundation.org
3. The National Entrepreneurship Network—www.nenindia.org
4. The Kauffman Foundation—www.kauffman.org
5. Stanford Technology Ventures Program University—www.stvp.stanford.edu
6. Stanford Entrepreneurship Network—www.sen.stanford.edu
7. Joel Barker's leadership videos—www.joelbarker.com

All trademarks referred to in this book are gratefully acknowledged.

Go Kiss the World
Life Lessons for the Young Professional

'Go, kiss the world' were Subroto Bagchi's blind mother's last words to him. These words became the guiding principle of his life.

Subroto Bagchi grew up amidst what he calls the 'material simplicity' of rural and small-town Orissa, imbibing from his family a sense of contentment, constant wonder, connectedness to a larger whole and learning from unusual sources. From humble beginnings, he went on to achieve extraordinary professional success, eventually co-founding MindTree, one of India's most admired software services companies.

Through personal anecdotes and simple words of wisdom, Subroto Bagchi brings to the young professional lessons in working and living, energizing ordinary people to lead extraordinary lives. *Go Kiss the World* will be an inspiration to 'young India', and to those who come from small-town India, teaching them to recognize and develop their inner strengths, thereby helping them realize their own, unique potential.

F/P0a008/7274/3/09